*The Carnegie
Conversation
on Catholic Education*

CATHOLIC EDUCATION STUDIES DIVISION

Alliance for Catholic Education Press
at the University of Notre Dame

The Carnegie Conversation on Catholic Education

Edited by
John Staud

ALLIANCE FOR CATHOLIC EDUCATION PRESS
AT THE UNIVERSITY OF NOTRE DAME

NOTRE DAME, INDIANA

Copyright © 2008

Alliance for Catholic Education Press
at the University of Notre Dame
158 I.E.I. Building
Notre Dame, IN 46556
http://www.nd.edu/~acepress

All rights reserved.

Cover and text design by Mary Jo Adams Kocovski

ISBN 978-0-9788793-3-4

"A Reflection by James Heft, S.M." is reprinted in part from "Responses From the Field" by James L. Heft, S.M., which appeared in *Catholic Education: A Journal of Inquiry & Practice, 11*(3), 320-325 © 2008 University of Notre Dame. Used with permission of the copyright owner.

Library of Congress Cataloging-in-Publication Data

The Carnegie conversation on Catholic education / edited by John Staud.
    p. cm.
  ISBN 978-0-9788793-3-4 (pbk. : alk. paper)
  1. Catholic Church--Education--United States. I. Staud, John J., 1965-
II. Carnegie Foundation for the Advancement of Teaching.

LC501.C28 2008
371.071'273--dc22
                                    2008031222

This book was printed on acid-free paper.
Printed in the United States of America

Table of Contents

Acknowledgment 5.

Introduction 6.
Tim Scully, C.S.C. and John Staud

Keynote Address and Responses

Preliminary Thoughts on Creating a Field as It Might Apply to Catholic Education 12.
Lee Shulman

A Response from Maureen Hallinan 15.

A Reponse from Gregory Aymond 18.

The Relevance of the Carnegie Conversation 21.
Ronald Nuzzi

Finding and Forming Teachers and Leaders

Presentation I: Shane Martin 24.

Presentation II: Karen Ristau 26.

Presentation III: John Convey 28.

Presentation IV: Ronald Nuzzi 31.

A Reflection by Patricia Helene Earl, I.H.M. 33.

A Reflection by Maureen Hackett 35.

A Reflection by Rosemary Croghan 37.

A Reflection by John Croghan 39.

Strengthening and Applying Scholarship on Religious Character and Academic Excellence

Presentation I: Daniel Lapsley 42.

Presentation II: Joseph O'Keefe, S.J. 47.

Presentation III: Lorraine Ozar 50.

Presentation IV: Mary Elizabeth Galt, B.V.M. 53.

A Reflection by Karen Ristau 56.

A Reflection by Timothy Cook 57.

A Reflection by Gerald Cattaro 59.

A Reflection by Tom Doyle 61.

A Reflection by James Heft, S.M. 62.

A Reflection by Martin Scanlan 64.

A Reflection by Mary Walsh and Jillian DePaul 66.

The Role of the Philanthropic Community in Strengthening and Sustaining Faith-Based Schools and Developing a Robust Field of Study

Presentation I: Francis Butler 70.

Presentation II: B.J. Cassin 72.

Presentation III: John Coons 74.

A Reflection by Maureen Hackett 77.

A Reflection by Darla Romfo 79.

A Reflection by Joshua Hale 80.

Innovative Models for Catholic School Renewal

A Reflection by Mary Diez, William Henk, and Martin Scanlan 84.

A Reflection by John Jordan 86.

Acknowledgment

The authors would like to thank both the current and former presidents of the Carnegie Foundation for the Advancement of Teaching, Tony Bryk and Lee Shulman, for convening and hosting the Carnegie Conversation on Catholic Education and for inspiring the many leaders in Catholic education in attendance and beyond to grow the field of Catholic education.

Introduction

Tim Scully, C.S.C. and John Staud

Although the United States has almost as many Catholic colleges and universities as the rest of the world combined, we have not been—as a collective—sufficiently energetic or imaginative in harnessing our considerable resources to serve the urgent needs of Catholic elementary and secondary schools in the United States.

Consider our own institution, the University of Notre Dame. We closed our Department of Education in the early 1970s, perhaps for good reasons and among them concerns that we were no longer providing a particularly distinctive contribution, but by doing so we absented ourselves from the most critical issue facing our nation's children, especially the poor, at a time of upheaval for many of the Catholic elementary and secondary schools that continued to serve these children so well. At the very moment when our nation's Catholic schools were entering their greatest crisis in their storied 200-hundred year history, Notre Dame ceased to contribute in a direct way. Fortunately, a number of Catholic universities did stay the course.

While it is true that most Catholic colleges and universities remained engaged in the field of education, it is also true that over the past 40 years, the majority of them, for all intents and purposes, lost focus on the specific needs of Catholic elementary and secondary schools for a new generation of well prepared faith-filled educators and for high quality research focused on Catholic schooling. Of our country's over 200 Catholic colleges and universities, only a few dozen now have programs—any program—to form teachers and leaders in the Catholic tradition specifically for the apostolate of Catholic education. And not all of these are degree-granting programs. As individual institutions and as a collective, we can do more and we can do better.

Notre Dame's absence spanned two decades until the founding of the Alliance for Catholic Education (ACE) in 1993. Perhaps curiously, having no department of education may have been a blessing in disguise, for the absence of an institutionally standard paradigm may have made it easier for Notre Dame to focus its renewed efforts more deliberately—and from the outset—exclusively on the needs of Catholic schools. From its inception, ACE flourished in large part because of partnerships with dioceses, schools, the National Catholic Educational Association (NCEA), the United States Conference of Catholic Bishops (USCCB), the Corporation for National and Community Service, and other universities, in particular the University of Portland, which educated the first four cohorts of ACE teachers until Notre Dame established its own Institute for Educational Initiatives and a set of highly focused graduate degree programs. It was this spirit of alliance that precipitated Notre Dame's response to the 2005 pastoral statement of the U.S. bishops, *Renewing Our Commitment to Catholic Elementary and Secondary Schools in the Third Millennium*. Notre Dame's president, Fr. John Jenkins convened a national task force to study the problem in depth and to make recommendations to the broader Church and for the University to deepen and expand its efforts.

At the very time that the Notre Dame task force was engaging in its study, Lee Shulman and three nationally known leaders in the field—Tony Bryk, Mary Diez, and Sharon Feimen-Nemser—spent a few days with us on campus providing strategic advice to the ACE organization. In this context, Shulman challenged us to advance Catholic education as a robust and vitally important field of study, both in and of itself as well as for the insights it might render on other faith-based schooling and public schooling. He argued persuasively that our capacity as universities to support K-12 Catholic schools depends to a great extent on our ability to re-imagine and invigorate a field of Catholic education. In keeping with his characteristic generosity, Shulman offered to host a national dialogue on these issues at the Carnegie Foundation for the Advancement of Teaching. His idea dovetailed neatly with the invitation of the bishops for Catholic higher education to do more to help elementary and secondary Catholic schools and the Task Force's call to "form partnerships [among] other Catholic colleges and universities" (2006, p. 9).

Recognizing finite resources and space, the planning committee and the supporting foundation sought to convene a diverse set of constituents representing higher education—Catholic, private, and public colleges and universities—as well as the NCEA, diocesan and other school systems, and members of the philanthropic community. Subtitled "Building a Movement and Strengthening a Field: The Revitalization of American Catholic Education," this fall 2007 conference convened approximately 50 participants in beautiful surroundings of the new facilities of the Carnegie Foundation in the hills of Palo Alto.

> *Our challenge and opportunity is to build this momentum through more systematic communication, collaboration, and broadened invitation to additional partners in order to maximize impact.*

The Carnegie dialogue explored a central governing question: What is a field and why is it important to strengthen the field of Catholic education? Shulman's opening keynote provided important arguments for the value of building a field. Subsequent panel discussions pursued three approaches to the question of how to strengthen this field, namely, forming teachers and leaders for Catholic schools, expanding and enhancing scholarship to improve the educational quality of Catholic schools, and ensuring the financial stability and accessibility of Catholic schools for students of today and tomorrow.

Originally, we planned that the Carnegie dialogue would serve as a foundation for three subsequent conferences designed to focus on each of these three approaches to strengthen the field and, thereby, the schools themselves. We were elated by the intense interest of our colleagues and partner institutions. Everyone invited expressed enthusiasm for the conference, and nearly everyone was able to participate. As acceptances mounted, Shulman even expressed some concern that we might exceed Carnegie's physical capacity! As we planned the agenda together with our many partners, our vision of what this opportunity might come to be and to mean continued to enlarge. Is it possible, we now wonder, that the Carnegie dialogue might come to be viewed, in time, as a moment blessed by Providence, one that brought together a community of scholars with a shared problematic—Catholic and faith-based education—and led to the deeper engagement and, in many cases, re-engagement of Catholic higher education in Catholic elementary and secondary schools?

Although participants at Carnegie recognized the serious challenges confronting Catholic schools, especially parochial schools in inner-city and rural areas, as in a real sense the underlying reason for the conference, there was a spirit of hope and energy fueled by recognition that Catholic schools have already displayed impressive resilience over the past 40 years as well as the conviction that a significant opportunity exists at this time to revitalize Catholic and faith-based schools throughout the United States. Enthusiasm for increased activity and collaboration proved to be an overarching theme, animated by the shared conviction that Catholic higher education has an essential role to play to ensure a bright future for Catholic elementary and secondary schools. There was also widespread agreement with Shulman's observation that the work going on at Catholic universities and colleges "needed to be better organized as a field of practice and scholarship, both for the benefit of Catholic institutions, but also for non-Catholic educators who could learn from research and dissemination of [such] work."

At Carnegie, participants came to realize that, among the dozen colleges and universities present, all are doing far more work on behalf of Catholic elementary and secondary schools than was the case ten, or even five years ago. Our challenge and opportunity is to build this momentum through more systematic communication, collaboration, and broadened invitation to additional partners in order to maximize impact. Concrete outcomes included the following:

First, we agreed to work together toward the development of a national database on Catholic schools, in order to be able to conduct urgently needed research on the outcomes of Catholic schools nationally. Rev. Joseph O'Keefe, S.J., Dean of the Lynch School of Education at Boston College, agreed to lead a working group, together with the NCEA and others, to develop this critical step to attract scholars to the study of Catholic education at the national level.

A second goal emerging from the Carnegie dialogue is to establish a special interest group (SIG) at the American Educational Research Association (AERA). AERA has numerous SIGs, but amazingly, there is none for the largest private, faith-based education system in the world. Of the thousands of presentations at the AERA annual meeting, few are specifically devoted to Catholic schools. Rev. Ronald Nuzzi, Director of the ACE Leadership Program at Notre Dame, and others are in pursuit of this designation as this document goes to print.

A third goal is to find ways to encourage more and better scholarship on Catholic and faith-based education. We need to attract resources to provide graduate fellowships and scholarships, post-doctoral positions, and recognition for learned study and influential research on the effectiveness of Catholic schools. Each institution committed itself to pursuing this objective, both individually and collectively.

Fourth, beginning with the publication and wide dissemination of the conference proceedings and through broader inclusion for subsequent activities and initiatives, we seek to attract more scholars and institutions to join this national effort. Going into Carnegie, the plan was to hold three follow-up conferences. Weeks later, the number had doubled, a sign of the opportunity as well as broad commitment to this agenda. To date, a conference-planning group representing eight institutions has articulated a plan to hold six follow-up conferences, two per year, with the hope being that additional institutions will propose and sponsor conferences in years to come.

1. Catholic Schools and the Immigrant Church: Lessons of the Past and Bridge to the Future
   January 2009 at Loyola Marymount (jointly sponsored with the University of San Francisco)
2. Forming Teachers and Leaders
   Spring 2009 at Loyola University Chicago
3. Enhancing Academic Excellence
   Fall 2009 at Boston College
4. Strengthening Catholic Identity
   Spring 2010 at The Catholic University of America
5. Facilitating Effective Structures and Governance
   Fall 2010 in Milwaukee (sponsored by Marquette University and Alverno College)
6. Ensuring Effective Stewardship
   Spring 2011 at the University of Notre Dame

These six conferences emerging from the initial conversation at Carnegie hold vital promise to catalyze a broader movement in Catholic higher education, as well as scholars at public, private, and faith-based colleges and universities, to study and serve Catholic and other faith-based elementary and secondary schools. Indeed, these eight Catholic colleges and universities have formed a partnership, for now named the Catholic Higher Education Collaborative (CHEC), to explore and develop collaborative initiatives in support of Catholic elementary and secondary schools in the United States. We hope that this partnership attracts many more colleges and universities, confident that our common agenda and spirit of collaboration will not only serve a vital need but will also enhance opportunities for scholarship, teaching, and service at participating institutions.

Hence this document, which seeks to disseminate the proceedings at Carnegie to a broader audience. Our monograph gathers the reflections of presenters and panelists on each of the three main themes that emerged. We are also pleased to include subsequent contributions from attendees and those who responded to a broader invitation to submit reflections on the proceedings at Carnegie. Moved by Pope Benedict's (2008) reminder during his recent visit to the United States that Catholic education "is an outstanding apostolate of hope," we take hope that the work begun at Carnegie will build momentum for a growing movement to strengthen Catholic elementary and secondary schools.

Rev. Tim Scully, C.S.C., Ph.D., is the Director of the Institute for Educational Initiatives at the University of Notre Dame.

John Staud, Ph.D., is the Director of Pastoral Formation and Administration for the University of Notre Dame's Alliance for Catholic Education.

Benedict XVI. (2008, April 17). *Remarks at The Catholic University of America*. Retrieved June 11, 2008, from http://publicaffairs.cua.edu/Releases/2008/PopeBenedictSpeech.cfm

Notre Dame Task Force on Catholic Education. (2006). *Making God known, loved, and served: The future of Catholic primary and secondary schools in America*. Notre Dame, IN: Author.

United States Conference of Catholic Bishops. (2005). *Renewing our commitment to Catholic elementary and secondary schools in the third millennium*. Washington, DC: Author.

Keynote Address

Preliminary Thoughts on Creating a Field
as it Might Apply to Catholic Education
Lee Shulman

This discussion began for me during a site visit to Notre Dame's ACE program as a member of a visiting committee with Mary Diez, Tony Bryk and Sharon Feimen-Nemser. As we were discussing this exciting program, we began to ask questions about ACE. We asked whether there was any evidence regarding the quality of the program beyond our casual observations about the impressiveness of the students, the commitment and energy of the faculty, the strong support of the institution and its leadership, and the broad range of urban areas in which ACE teachers are privileged to teach. We also asked whether there were other places where similar programs were underway from which Notre Dame and the ACE folks could learn. We were beginning to ask whether there was a robust field of Catholic education—teaching, teacher preparation, professional development, quality assessment, general and specific scholarship, methods of exchanging ideas, questions, findings, analyses and corrections.

Our colleagues described how other Catholic universities were also engaged in important initiatives in Catholic education, especially as relevant to the challenges of teaching in urban settings. We asked how often folks from those institutions came together to exchange experiences, scholarship, difficulties and epiphanies. We at Carnegie have worked with faculty and administrators from Catholic institutions of higher education in the areas of doctoral education, education in the professions of law, medicine, nursing, engineering, and the clergy (including the education of priests in seminaries), in undergraduate liberal education and in the role of colleges and universities in educating for civic and political engagement in a democracy. But we have not asked this particular question.

What Are Some of the Attributes of a Field?

A field engages in knowledge building, institution building, and the education of individuals. It is organized into communities of scholarship and practice. It has developed ways of organizing knowledge, criticizing knowledge claims and "growing" its knowledge base. It has developed ways of dealing with uncertainty, disagreements and controversy. It has a sense of who peers are, and therefore who has the standing to deal with questions of warrant, validity, value and advancement. A field develops ways of judging and controlling quality—the quality of knowledge claims, the quality of aspiring and veteran practitioners. A field usually has an institutional presence, whether in academic departments, schools, interdisciplinary centers or outside the boundaries of academic institutions in distinct organizations like independent seminaries or think tanks.

Imagine that the following are some of the distinctive features of a field: One of the features of a field is some sense of a body of knowledge, along with processes needed to critique knowledge claims, to add and subtract from bodies of knowledge, to synthesize, review and organize knowledge and to connect knowledge to other bodies of understanding and to domains of practice. This knowledge is understood as belonging to a field in general, not just in the minds and experience of individual practitioners or institutions. Does Catholic education aspire to that kind of knowledge base? How would it relate to more general conceptions of knowledge in education, teaching, learning, development or formation?

Mapping a Field

A field is a topographical metaphor, a metaphor of place, location, cartography. Can you draw a map of the field? How it is internally divided? What are the relative sizes of the constituent parts? How are they configured?

What are the domains on the borders of this field? What are Catholic education's closest neighbors in disciplinary and professional terms? How do these domains interact within institutions? Across and among institutions?

In terms of institutional place, where do we locate Catholic education?

In terms of institutional place, where do we locate Catholic education? Does it belong in the realm of the social sciences, with sociology, psychology, human development, anthropology? Do we imagine the emergence of a "science" of Catholic education? In the humanities with philosophy, theology, literature or history? Is Catholic education a field of professional education, more like medical, nursing or social work education?

What are the primary intellectual achievements of the field? What does it mean to know Catholic education as a professor? To what extent are there discoveries, insights, inventions, analyses or normative claims of the field itself, and to what extent do they derive from neighboring fields such as theology, history, Scripture, homiletics, apologetics, ethics, sociology, cultural studies, linguistics, Semitics, etc? How are the intellectual accomplishments of a scholar of Catholic education different from those of someone competent to practice in the field? How are they different from any other successful urban educator?

What are the primary practical achievements of the field? What are the skills, practices, and techniques needed for playing the role of a Catholic educator?

What are the primary moral, ethical and personal qualities that require professional formation in someone who can function as a Catholic educator?

Do programs study their own practice? Are there other places doing similar things? Do they learn from one another's practice? Do they engage in research or evaluation? Do they exchange findings? From whom do they recruit? Inside the club? Outside the club? What's the club?

If you were committed to building a powerful faculty in Catholic education for your university or college, where would you look to recruit? Other Catholic universities, and if so, in which departments or programs? Secular universities, and if so, same question. Successful Catholic schools? None of the above?

How are the following distinguished from one another? A Catholic educator and an educator in any other community, discipline or profession? A Catholic educator and a Catholic priest, nurse or counselor?

Concluding Assertions

If Catholic education is to become a robust field of scholarship and practice, it cannot be of interest only "within the club," that is, within Catholic educational institutions. A truly robust field will be studied in non-Catholic institutions, both private and public, and will thus be both tested and deliberated about among the broader communities of scholars and practitioners. If the field is asking appropriately "big questions" it cannot be developed in a parochial manner.

If Catholic education is to become a robust field, it must help develop a broader field of both general and tradition-specific religious education/formation. Without strong fields of Jewish education, Muslim education, Lutheran education and the like—or more likely, the unlike—Catholic education is likely to have limited opportunities for becoming robust.

If Catholic education is to become a robust field, it must become a robust field of scholarship—including scholarships of teaching and learning, of discovery and invention, of integration, connectedness and meaning, and of application and translation.

> *If Catholic education is to become a robust field, it will have to be vigorously, self-consciously and outrageously interdisciplinary.*

This scholarship must ask questions of application and practical efficacy, a scholarship of teaching and learning—both within the higher education institutions and in the schools and other settings in which Catholic education operates for children and families.

This scholarship must include basic studies of the disciplinary sort—the conditions for religious and character formation; the investigation of conceptions of faith and belief; theological studies of God and man; historical studies of schooling and socialization.

If Catholic education is to become a robust field, it will have to be vigorously, self-consciously and outrageously interdisciplinary. It will need to be pursued in new forms of academic organization, such as centers, committees, institutes or professional schools that creatively integrate and congregate leading scholars and wise practitioners in the service of Catholic education and formation.

If Catholic education is to become a robust field, it cannot staff itself overwhelmingly by borrowing, stealing or seducing faculty from other fields. It must ultimately develop robust programs of scholarly and professional formation through longer-term academic preparation with Catholic education as its professional and scholarly focus.

If Catholic education is to become a robust field, it needs to attend to all three apprenticeships of professional and higher learning—apprenticeships of thought, of practice and of the spirit—leading to habits of mind, habits of practice and habits of the heart. And its preparation programs must reflect the attributes associated with powerful professional and scholarly formation, what Anne Colby (2006) has called "enactment," "embodiment," and "dailiness."

If Catholic education is to become a robust field, it needs to develop mature networks of professional communication, collaboration, critique and high quality review so that the knowledge base of the field exceeds the knowledge acquired from research, practice or normative analysis conducted at any one institution in within one association or community. Our mantra at Carnegie is that we have three rules of engagement in a robust field with respect to experiments of thought, action or normation.

Lee Shulman, Ph.D., is the President of the Carnegie Foundation for the Advancement of Teaching.

Make it public; critically review it; pass it on.

Colby, A. (2006, December). *The formation of professionalism in medical, nursing, and engineering education.* Paper presented at the Notre Dame Symposium on Personality and Moral Character, Notre Dame, IN.

A Response from Maureen Hallinan

Lee Shulman's thought-provoking essay in this volume raises important and timely questions about a field of Catholic education. First, he identifies the components of a field: knowledge production, institution building, and practice. Then he distinguishes between a field and an academic discipline and indicates that the study and practice of education should be regarded as a field, not a discipline. Finally, he raises what is the most important question for our purposes, namely, whether we should regard Catholic education as a field and, if so, how we can build and strengthen it.

Shulman points out that the function of an academic discipline is knowledge building and transmission. A field is broader than an academic discipline. In addition to creating a knowledge base, a field is concerned with an institution's role and with the application of knowledge to practice.

Even though knowledge production is the bedrock of both a field and an academic discipline, they differ in a fundamental way in how they treat knowledge building. Academic disciplines formulate theoretical models that provide a unique perspective on their area of interest. Ideally, a field would do the same. In practice, however, fields typically borrow theoretical models from the academic disciplines rather than develop their own unique intellectual foundations. For example, the field of social work relies on theories from sociology, psychology, economics and other social sciences to pose and answer research questions and interpret the results of data analyses. Similarly, the field of education relies mostly on social science theories to generate and test propositions about educational processes.

Catholic education must develop its own intellectual base, formulating theories that utilize extant work in theology and the social sciences.

Examples of the way educational researchers utilize academic disciplines to inform their studies are numerous. They use sociological theories of status attainment to explain educational attainment. They rely on psychological theories of motivation and sociological and political science theories of racial, ethnic and class inequality to understand the achievement gap. Educational researchers turn to the sociology of organizations and to social psychological theories about human development and authority to understand the effects of institutional and organizational structure. They employ political science theories of power, conflict, compromise, values and ideology to analyze curriculum content and evaluate instructional practices. In addition, they utilize tools and models developed in psychometrics and statistics to assess educational outcomes, such as standardized tests and grades.

The absence of a unique theoretical foundation is a significant shortcoming for a field. Without a set of theories that explain the basic processes of interest, researchers will obtain only limited insights into the determinants and consequences of their practices and policies. Since the field of education has yet to build a rich theoretical foundation to inform and guide its intellectual pursuits, it has been slow to accumulate a systematic body of empirical research that would generate new theoretical insights and inform the choice of future empirical research studies. A lack of theory about educational processes also explains why the findings and interpretation of educational research are often inconsistent across studies and criticized for lacking validity and reliability.

16.

The theoretical limitations of education scholarship are one of the factors that account for the low status of departments and schools of education in institutions of higher learning. The status difference between faculty in education and those in traditional academic disciplines may be evident in noting the lower salaries and slower promotion rates of those in education. Administrators at many institutions view departments of education as teacher training programs or professional schools and not as knowledge generators. As a result, their programs lack the status conferred on academic disciplines whose contribution to knowledge is generally taken for granted. The low status of education in institutions of higher learning translates into fewer college and university resources to build scholarship, conduct research and improve practice.

At the same time, the fact that education is a field rather than an academic discipline provides certain advantages. First, education researchers and practitioners have access to federal, state, and private funding specifically targeted for educational research, professional development, and curricular innovation. These funds typically are not available to scholars outside the field of education. Second, education is not constrained by the rigid intellectual boundaries that characterize most academic disciplines. Education is free to be interdisciplinary in a way that academic disciplines are not. Pointing out the value of interdisciplinary scholarship, Shulman urges educators to be "vigorously, self-consciously and outlandishly" interdisciplinary. Finally, educators, as opposed to academic scholars, can focus on institution building and practice as well as knowledge creation. This broader range of interests provides them with the satisfaction of contributing directly to the social, moral, and ethical dimensions of human development as well as the cognitive dimension of learning.

Building a Field of Catholic Education

The question remains whether Catholic education can and should be regarded as a field distinct from general education. Shulman's essay suggests that Catholic education has the potential to become a field, but first, it needs to be built and strengthened. Like any field, Catholic education must rest on a solid body of knowledge. However, like general education, the theories that Catholic educators currently employ to explain educational processes have been formulated by scholars who are concerned about diverse social phenomena other than education. Catholic education must develop its own intellectual base, formulating theories that utilize extant work in theology and the social sciences. It must identify and conceptualize the unique processes that operate in Catholic schools and explain the mechanisms that govern the influence of Catholic education on the development of children and adults. A systematic analysis and synthesis of existing research on Catholic education would contribute to the foundation of a field of Catholic education.

General education is recognized as a legitimate area of study in most colleges and universities. At present, students who take courses in Catholic education may obtain course credit toward a general education degree, but are not awarded a degree or even a specialization in Catholic education. To build a distinct field of Catholic education, faculty must be hired specifically for this purpose. Moreover, as part of an academic program, Catholic education needs an institutional presence. The program must be part of the organizational structure of a university, by becoming a school, department, institute, center, or other institutional unit. The program must meet university requirements and standards for award-

Building a field of Catholic education ultimately involves creating communities of scholars at universities who will conduct research and offer degree programs in Catholic education.

ing Master's and doctoral degrees and for teacher training programs and teacher certification.

The courses offered in a Catholic education degree program will differ fundamentally from courses in general education. Faculty must develop a theoretically strong, faith-based curriculum in Catholic education. The program would not simply add courses in religion or religious studies to the general education curriculum. A Catholic education curriculum would be characterized by the infusion of a faith-vision into all its courses.

Since the ultimate purpose of knowledge building is knowledge transmission, students working toward a degree in Catholic education must be prepared to teach in K-12 Catholic schools. These future Catholic educators need to learn how to express and teach their faith, norms and values through the K-12 curriculum. For example, they could be shown how a social studies course might include a discussion of Catholic teaching on social justice and how a biology course could include a discussion of the sanctity of human life. Or, in lieu of specifically discussing religious beliefs in their courses, future Catholic school teachers could be prepared to highlight the religious environment of a Catholic school as part of their instructional mission.

Recent social science research can contribute to the building of a field of Catholic education. James Coleman (1982), Tony Bryk (1993), and their colleagues found that students in Catholic schools attained higher test scores than those in public schools. They attributed this "Catholic school advantage," in part, to the communal organization of Catholic schools. Researchers and students of Catholic education can build on these important findings to investigate the processes, both faith-based and scientific, that produce these results. Future Catholic school teachers can learn how to utilize the benefits of community life to promote students' religious, cognitive, social, and moral development.

Building a field of Catholic education ultimately involves creating communities of scholars at universities who will conduct research and offer degree programs in Catholic education. It also involves forming communities of teachers and learners in Catholic elementary and secondary schools. These efforts will be motivated and enriched by Catholic faith and practice. The United States Conference of Catholic Bishops (2005) states that Catholic schools provide "an atmosphere in which the Gospel message is proclaimed, community in Christ is experienced, service to our sisters and brothers is the norm...thanksgiving and worship of our God is cultivated." More broadly defined, this is the mission and goal of a field of Catholic education.

Maureen Hallinan, Ph.D., is the White Professor of Sociology and Director of the Center for Research on Educational Opportunity in the Institute for Educational Initiatives at the University of Notre Dame.

Bryk, A., Lee, V., & Holland, P. (1993). *Catholic schools and the common good.* Cambridge, MA: Harvard University Press.
Coleman, J., Hoffer, T., & Kilgore, S. (1982). *High school achievement: Public, Catholic and private schools compared.* New York: Basic Books.
United States Conference of Catholic Bishops. (2005). *Renewing our commitment to Catholic elementary and secondary schools in the third millennium.* Washington, DC: Author.

A Response from Gregory Aymond

Thank you for the opportunity to be part of this important conversation on Catholic education. I am pleased to respond to Lee Shulman's presentation. For my response I would like to raise five questions for our discussion.

First, I believe Shulman gives a compelling argument in favor of establishing a field of Catholic education. I agree with him that this field must interface with other fields of study, including sociology, psychology, Christian anthropology, philosophy, literature and theology. However, I propose that this field must interface with the study of religious education and theology but, at the same time, be a field of its own. For the sake of our conversation, I wish to name it "faith formation." The ministry of Catholic education involves not only the sharing of knowledge in many subjects, including theology, but also invites and challenges our young people to be formed in faith.

This conversation can and should take place with other faiths, religions and Christian denominations. At the same time, we cannot simply adopt their programs because there is something unique about Catholic education. Therefore, it is evident that this conversation and scholarship established in the field of Catholic education must move forward. My question? Who has the interest, the power and the influence to do so? Who is going to take the risk and to place forward both personnel and financial resources to create this field and to begin this conversation and scholarship? Who will do it and will we be participants in this important discussion?

The mission of Catholic education is to provide excellence in education, excellence in religious education and theology and excellence in faith formation and evangelization.

Second, sometimes in our Church we are better at competition than collaboration. I have heard from many of you, and have experienced for myself, that there is competition among some Catholic colleges and universities. A question that this conversation places before us: how can we collaborate in a way that will strengthen Catholic education in the United States and become for us an even greater gift? Who will bring these 225 colleges and universities and help them to develop an understanding of and appreciation for and commitment to Catholic education? Can the Association of Catholic Colleges and Universities (ACCU) be an agent? Can the National Catholic Educational Association (NCEA) be an important partner in this conversation?

We all know that there are Catholic colleges and universities who have an education department and yet are not in any way connected to the Church at large or a diocese in striving to foster Catholic schools and Catholic identity. What can we do to make sure that all Catholic colleges and schools, who have an education department, make a strong commitment to forming teachers for Catholic schools? As our teachers are formed in faith, or given the opportunity to be formed in faith, they will be able to hand on the faith to others. I remember a meeting with a dean of the school of education in a particular university and suggesting that their department reach out and provide particular service to Catholic school teachers, helping them to establish Catholic identity and making a direct connection in supplying teachers for Catholic schools. In this particular diocese the response was, "We never really thought of that." I dare say that we all know of schools like that. What can we do to invite them to sit at the table with us and to be collaborators? What can we do to make sure that we are not competing but truly collaborating?

Third, this morning we spoke about value proposition and what we are driven by in Catholic education. May I take the opportunity to focus the question a little bit differently? What is the mission of Catholic education? It is the mission of

Christ, to teach as he did. The mission of Catholic education is to provide excellence in education, excellence in religious education and theology, and excellence in faith formation and evangelization.

One of the greatest gifts of the Catholic Church to the United States has been Catholic schools and the Catholic school system. We said earlier today that many of our adults do not understand their role as the primary educators of their children and certainly do not understand their vocation as faith formators. Perhaps in our adult education programs and parishes and in dioceses we can use this as an opportunity to share with them their important vocation as teachers and faith formators of their children and introduce them into the mission of Catholic education and Catholic schools. What can we do to make sure that our mission remains focused, that of excellence in education, religious education, theology and faith formation? Faith formation is different from the education that we provide in many different subjects and even religious education. It is our mission to form our young people in the ways of the Lord and to help them to grow in a deeper understanding of their relationship with Jesus and how they can grow in his life and love and be active members of our faith community. How can we keep this as our central focus?

Fourth, have we allowed the Catholic education system to become weakened? Unintentionally, we have I believe due to several reasons but I will limit this conversation to two.

1. We have placed in important leadership positions in our Catholic schools, particularly the roles of president, principal and other significant administrative roles, people who have been trained and even well trained in the public school system but do not understand the mission of Catholic education and have had no prior experience or training in Catholic education. We need a field to train these people before they assume these important leadership responsibilities. We need a field to be able to provide scholarships and training for those who would like to respond to the call of leadership in Catholic schools as their vocation.

2. How else have we weakened our Catholic education system? By the cost. We all know that this is a very complicated question. However, there are many people who would like to take advantage of Catholic schools and are not able to afford them. This is an issue of social justice and one which we cannot afford to leave unnoticed or unanswered. There is no easy answer. At the same time, we must continue to work vigorously for school choice. Perhaps some of us have gotten tired of this conversation and of this fight. I know even for myself in the last legislative session in Texas I was asked to testify before the Senate Committee on School Choice. I went, I gave my testimony and I did so with conviction and vigor but I must go to confession to you, publicly, and admit that on the way to the capitol I wondered, "Is this worth it?" We cannot become hopeless. We must continue to be leaders with energy, drawing on God's enlightenment and his spirits. What can we do to make sure that we do not continue to weaken our Catholic education ministry within our country and beyond?

Fifth, what does a leader in Catholic education look like? What kind of person are we describing? I am not suggesting that each person in every classroom will have all of these qualifications but I am suggesting that as we look at establishing a field of Catholic education that we have to ask the question: Who are we trying to help? What outcome do we expect? Certainly, our leaders in Catholic education, principals and other key administrators should possess the following eight qualities.

1. They would be a person of faith and one who actively lives and values their Catholic faith.
2. The administrators of our schools would lead the faculty, students and their families as a true and strong leader in faith.
3. They must be creative educators.
4. They must be very knowledgeable in Catholic theology and have had adequate courses in Catholic theology.
5. In order to be a Catholic educator, they must be strong leaders.
6. They must possess the ability to be a strong collaborator with others at the local, diocesan, and national levels.
7. These leaders in Catholic education must have a fundamental option for the poor, those who are economically poor as well as the poor in spirit.
8. Finally, these leaders would see their work not just as a job or responsibility but as a ministry. We would hope that they would be able to see this as a call from God sharing in the ministry of the Church. We need to form them and train them as lay ecclesial ministers, as co-workers with the ordained ministry and others in lay ministry.

I think there are several compelling arguments for establishing and promoting a field of Catholic education. In order to accomplish this we must work together and think creatively. We must draw on the wisdom and the enlightenment of our God who is truly the one who gives us knowledge and truth. We must teach as Jesus did and in order to do so we must follow his way. I believe that he will certainly walk with us in not only asking these questions but in finding answers that will strengthen and promote Catholic education in the Catholic Church and in our nation.

[
Most Reverend Gregory Aymond is Bishop of the Diocese of Austin, Texas.
]

The Relevance of the Carnegie Conversation

Ronald Nuzzi

As if to affirm the importance of the fall 2007 gathering at Carnegie, Catholic education has repeatedly been in the national spotlight during the 2007-2008 academic year. Federal and state legislators as well as Church leaders continue to grapple with issues of educational policy, large scale school closures continue to mount, national political leaders have been lavish in their praise of Catholic schools, the presence of charter schools continues to challenge and threaten Catholic schools, and Pope Benedict XVI reserved one day of his visit to the United States to address Catholic university presidents and diocesan superintendents.

> *The next few years will be critical in stemming the tide of school closings, helping existing schools excel, strengthening Catholic identity, improving academic programming, and reaching consensus on a best practices approach to the administration and management of the Catholic educational system.*

The Carnegie Conversation could not have happened at a better time. Underscoring the gravity of the precipitous and ongoing decline in national Catholic school enrollment, the Diocese of Rochester, New York, announced in January 2008 that 13 of 24 Catholic schools in Monroe County, the seat of the 12-county diocese, would close at the end of the school year. In the same month, the Archdiocese of Washington, DC, announced that it was preparing to downsize its Center City Consortium, a decade-old "diocese-within-a-diocese" governance structure that supported the networking, resource sharing, and common curriculum of 12 schools in the inner city. The new consortium will have only four schools. More troubling, however, was the plan to take seven of the schools and turn them into public charter schools. If successful, this would mark the first time that such a large scale "conversion" of Catholic schools into public schools has occurred. While many parishes and dioceses rent former school facilities to charter corporations or a public school district, no diocese heretofore has attempted a single conversion of such magnitude. While the archdiocese is hoping to keep the displacement of children and families to a minimum, many have wondered about the effect such an approach will have nationwide, and if other dioceses will follow suit.

During the State of Union, President Bush called for the establishment of Pell Grants for Kids, a clever phrase drawing attention to the fact that federal dollars are provided for tuition support for students enrolled in private colleges and universities, but these funds are never available to students in private K-12 schooling. Thus college freshmen at any religiously affiliated college or university in the country have access to federal grants and loans in the form of Pell Grants to help fund their college education. But one year earlier, when such students were high school seniors, such federal funding would not be available to them were they enrolled in a religious school. Hence the president's felicitous term: Pell Grants for Kids. While appreciated by those in private education, the president's budget request of $300 million to fund such grants for students trapped in failing public schools fell on deaf, if not hostile ears in the Democratic controlled Congress.

Even as momentum builds, challenges continue to grow and multiply.

The president also called for a spring 2008 White House Summit in response to the steady decline of faith-based schools in the inner city. Though he did not mention Catholic schools specifically, his aim could not have been clearer. The day after the State of the Union address, U.S. Secretary of Education Margaret Spelling said, "Catholic schools are treasures, especially in our cities, but their numbers are in decline." And the day after that, First Lady of the United States, Mrs. Laura Bush, visited a Catholic school in Washington, DC, not far from her home, and praised the commitment of parents, faculty, students, clergy, and community leaders in working to sustain a vital Catholic and educational presence in the heart of the nation's capital.

Even as momentum builds, challenges continue to grow and multiply. The proposed conferences recently committed to by the Carnegie attendees will go a long way to bring about solutions to the policy, governance, financial, and leadership challenges facing Catholic schools. The next few years will be critical in stemming the tide of school closings, helping existing schools excel, strengthening Catholic identity, improving academic programming, and reaching consensus on a best practices approach to the administration and management of the Catholic educational system.

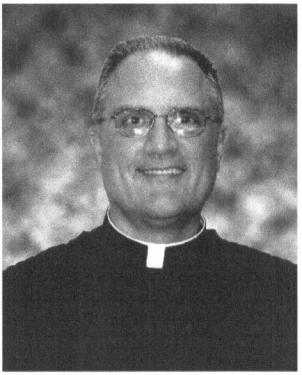

Rev. Ronald Nuzzi, Ph.D., is the Director of the Alliance for Catholic Education's (ACE) Leadership Program at the University of Notre Dame and Editor of *Catholic Education: A Journal of Inquiry & Practice.*

Finding and Forming
Teachers and Leaders

Presentation I: Shane Martin

The education of today's youth is of major importance to the Church as well as to society. The United States Conference of Catholic Bishops (USCCB) have addressed this issue in a series of pastoral letters (1990, 1995, 2005) and makes clear in their 2005 letter that it is the responsibility of the entire Church to work towards the goal of making Catholic elementary and secondary schools available, accessible, and affordable to all Catholic parents and their children. As the bishops state, "all Catholics must join together in efforts to ensure that Catholic schools have administrators and teachers who are prepared to provide an exceptional educational experience for young people—one that is both truly Catholic and of the highest academic quality" (USCCB, 2005, p. 1). Catholic colleges and universities have a special obligation to contribute to the education of PreK-12 students. The bishops call upon Catholic higher education to provide a sufficient number of programs of the highest quality to recruit and prepare school administrators and teachers so that they are knowledgeable in matters of faith, are professionally prepared, and are committed to the Church (USCCB, 2005).

In order to meet the challenges of fulfilling the role envisioned by the bishops, Catholic higher education must be innovative and entrepreneurial in its approach to preparing teachers and principals. One traditional hallmark of Catholic education has been its emphasis on local decision making and site-based management. Teachers and principals in Catholic schools wear multiple hats in responding to the educational needs of their students, and they do so unencumbered by a large, bureaucratic district structure that dictates an overly centralized approach to instruction and learning. Catholic educator preparation programs must be of high quality and also meet the unique needs of their students. Colleges and universities that offer these programs need to consider the value they add to distinguish themselves from other programs. In addition to addressing pedagogical issues, programs should also prepare teachers to plan across the curriculum, to understand their role as teacher-leaders, and to work effectively with the various stakeholders in the education process. In addition to instructional leadership, principals need preparation in business planning, human resources, private school law, development, and stewardship. The preparation of Catholic educators needs to happen in the context of faith formation and spirituality.

The preparation of Catholic educators needs to happen in the context of faith formation and spirituality.

Partnerships with local (arch)diocesan departments of Catholic schools are also very important. Universities can partner in creative and innovative ways to support local efforts. For example, at Loyola Marymount University in Los Angeles, we have partnered with the archdiocese to form a number of programs. Our PLACE program (Partners in Los Angeles Catholic Education) is our ACE-like program that is a part of the UCCE network. In its eighth year we have now graduated over 100 Catholic school teachers with approximately 80% continuing to serve in Catholic schools beyond their two-year commitment. We have partnership programs in Catholic inclusive education (special education), principal development, literacy, and we are creating a new early childhood program. Our LMU/LA CAST program (Catholic Archdiocesan School Teachers) is an innovative Saturday program that features hybrid on-line courses. We also have an option in our doctoral program, the Ed.D. in Leadership for Social Justice, that is specifically for Catholic school leadership.

Catholic colleges and universities can also provide capacity for researching best practices and achievements in Catholic education. There are several important research studies conducted since the 1970s and much more recent anecdotal evidence that Catholic schools provide an advantage for life, especially for inner-city and poorer children. We need to add to this body of literature and document our successes and engage in dialogue with researchers from public and charter school education.

In doing the above work, Catholic colleges and universities should pay special attention to two important issues: the growing diversity of the Church and the inclusion of technology in training programs. As Catholic educators, we must be active in our stance to recruit and retain diverse faculty in our universities and diverse students in our programs. The diversity of the Church should be reflected in the diversity of programs and their faculty. Technology can assist in delivering quality, innovative programs that model best practices in this area for teachers and principals. Attention to diversity and technology should characterize Catholic education programs.

There are many opportunities for Catholic colleges and universities in providing service to Catholic education programs. Following the best traditions of Catholic education, these programs must be creative, innovative, and engaging. Catholic universities can play an important leadership role in guaranteeing the future of Catholic K-12 education. The entire educational pipeline—elementary, secondary, and higher education—needs to work together for sustained success. As the bishops remind us, now is the time.

Shane Martin, Ph.D., is Dean of the School of Education at Loyola Marymount University.

United States Catholic Conference. (1990). *In support of Catholic elementary and secondary schools*. Washington, DC: Author.
United States Catholic Conference. (1995). *Principles for educational reform in the United States*. Washington, DC: Author.
United States Conference of Catholic Bishops. (2005). *Renewing our commitment to Catholic elementary and secondary schools in the third millennium*. Washington, DC: Author.

Presentation II: Karen Ristau

First, I believe the two roles named in this question should be separated in order to adequately address the issue. While some basic commonalities for anyone working in the Catholic school system certainly do exist, there are different paths for the "finding" part of this question and additional knowledge and skills for those serving as leaders. We might suppose the need to find new teachers assumes they are not yet in the system, but we would prefer to think those preparing for leadership positions would already be serving in Catholic education—or at least come with the experience of teaching. In other words, not novices in education.

In my remarks I will address the question as it pertains to leaders. To explore the more precise question, how will people be found and prepared for the leadership roles in Catholic education, I will define the issues as I see them, discuss who is attending to the issue at present, and then suggest what colleges and universities can do beyond programs to establish Catholic education as a field of study.

Framing the Issue

While there are many excellent people serving Catholic education in a variety of roles across the country, there is a shortage of well-prepared persons able and willing to accept leadership positions. At the present time, two large dioceses are still without superintendents for two years running and another will go looking soon. In a nationwide think-tank in which over one hundred National Catholic Educational Association (NCEA) members from across the country participated, the need for leaders and good leadership emerged as the highest priority. Through my own observations and conversations, I would say the concern is well placed. Generous and good-hearted but unprepared persons accept school principalships more often in parish elementary schools than in secondary schools. Hiring persons with only public school experience, which happens more at the secondary level and at the diocesan level, is seen as weakening the Catholic identity of the enterprise. More often than not, hiring unprepared persons, in other words—any one will do—sends a covert message which promotes a culture of mediocrity and which undermines the aims of Catholic education.

> *…hiring unprepared persons, in other words—any one will do—sends a covert message which promotes a culture of mediocrity and which undermines the aims of Catholic education.*

Very effective leaders, particularly in secondary school, are not willing to serve as superintendents for two reasons: they would be paid less and would have less autonomy in a central office. Leadership positions are perceived to be fraught with tension headaches and the work is seen as undesirable.

The challenge to foster large numbers of people at all levels who are well prepared includes the problem of how to make the ministry of administration an attractive one. Catholic education will not fulfill the promise it holds without excellent leadership and without solving these questions.

The way in which leadership definitions are framed and concomitant issues considered will influence what is done. Leadership in itself is a messy business—much like life. It is neither linear nor sure; it is filled with surprise situations, which throw one off guard. It is not an exact science. The answers, solutions and recipes learned in graduate schools are necessary but insufficient. Preparation programs are correct to include courses in law, finance, supervision of personnel, curriculum design and so on as applicable in the setting of a Catholic school. And moreover ought to include some thoughtful theology courses. Yet, one cannot be completely prepared for every contingency which walks through the office door. To be better prepared for the unforeseen, I would suggest a critically important ability for leadership is the capacity to think broadly, to ask deeper questions, to act out of a carefully conceptualized sense of educational purpose and from a firmly held belief that this work is part of building the Kingdom of God. Thoughtful degree programs and insightful on-going education can provide a leader with these abilities.

Attending to the Issue

At the present time, there are over 40 Catholic colleges and universities which offer degree and certificate programs for Catholic educational leaders. The extent to which the programs focus specifically on Catholic education varies. While many operate programs with limited resources and nominal support, most have found innovative ways to address issues of cost and delivery. The colleges and universities are gathered in a loosely structured organization, the Association of Catholic Leadership Programs. Their purpose is to support one another, share program information and work to improve Catholic leadership preparation. These institutions deserve commendations for their work. While much good has been accomplished, much remains to be done.

> *The challenge to foster large numbers of people at all levels who are well prepared includes the problem of how to make the ministry of administration an attractive one.*

What Colleges and Universities Can Do

In thinking about promoting Catholic education as a field of study, I would recommend colleges and universities do what higher education does well and which no other institution can do: offer cohesive degree programs and produce new knowledge through scholarly work.

That said, I would offer a few ideas. I would challenge those who undertake the task of preparing leaders for Catholic education to review programs with attention to the Catholic intellectual tradition. A phenomenological study or more qualitative studies of what principals and superintendents actually do in their positions could inform preparation programs. Studies such as these could lead to better congruency between theory and practice.

In order to attract potential leaders, new scholarship is needed to explore and promote the understanding of Catholic educational leadership as a vocation, incorporating some of the theology found in the recent United States Conference of Catholic Bishops (USCCB, 2005) document, *Coworkers in the Vineyard of the Lord*.

Research shows people choose to be leaders because they are inspired by what they perceive about present leaders. Leaders who do their work with energy, enthusiasm and in a spirit of hopefulness will pass on by infection an interest in leadership (Fullen, 2001). To present the role of leader as a more attractive one, researchers in Catholic colleges and universities could produce studies which reveal what actually is accomplished by principals and by superintendents and find role models to emulate.

Finally, the most important contribution of continuing to develop Catholic education as a field of study is its promise to raise the intellectual level of the enterprise and acknowledge the value of the life of the mind—a long held treasure of Catholic education.

Fullen, M. (2001). *Leading in a culture of change*. San Francisco: Jossey-Bass.
United States Conference of Catholic Bishops. (2005). *Coworkers in the vineyard of the Lord*. Washington, DC: Author.

Karen Ristau, Ed.D., became NCEA's ninth president in July 2005.

Presentation III: John Convey

Importance of Leadership

Leadership is the key to the success of effective Catholic schools. Leadership at the diocesan level falls first and foremost to the bishop and subsequently to the superintendent of Catholic schools; at the parish level, to the pastors whose parishes have responsibility for schools; and at the school level, to the principals. When good leadership is in place, schools thrive. Problematic leadership has drastic consequences—some immediate, some delayed. Leadership becomes increasingly more important as the schools strive to offer a quality academic and religious education in the face of increasing costs. Poor leadership is often devastating to Catholic schools, particularly to those schools located in the inner city of large urban areas because of their fragile financial circumstances.

Permit me to cite just a few notable past examples of leadership in Catholic education. Exemplary leadership was shown by:
- Dennis Cardinal Dougherty, Archbishop of Philadelphia, who from 1918 to 1951 built the Catholic school system so that every Catholic child could attend a parish elementary school or diocesan high school, free of charge.
- James Cardinal Hickey, who said "I will not abandon the city" when he established the Center City Consortium of Catholic inner-city schools in the Archdiocese of Washington in 1997.
- Shirley Bougere, a principal from Baton Rouge, Louisiana, and a doctoral student in the program in Catholic educational leadership at The Catholic University of America, who immediately after Katrina wrote: "I spent the past few days registering students who are displaced from the New Orleans area. My school went from 299 students to 350 in two hours. We are now at 469. I have opened 7 new sections and hired 8 new teachers. We are conducting classes in every nook and cranny in this school. My teachers are troopers, not one complaint, even with all of their own problems."
- Bishop Thomas Rodi, who in the aftermath of Hurricane Katrina's devastation of six Catholic schools and ten churches along the Gulf Coast of Mississippi moved quickly with the cooperation of state and federal officials to build St. Patrick High School, a new Catholic high school serving the Diocese of Biloxi, the first school built in Mississippi since Katrina.

Challenges

I will mention two significant challenges in leadership succession that Catholic schools face. The first challenge is the transition from religious to lay leadership, a well-recognized trend noted in the report of the Notre Dame Task Force on Catholic Education (2006). Superintendents and principals from religious communities benefited from their formation and experience in Catholic schools and from the supervision and support that they received from their religious communities. Dioceses and individual schools must be more aggressive in identifying individuals for leadership positions and in preparing them for their roles.

Unlike their public school counterparts, Catholic school superintendents and principals have to "do it all" often with little administrative and professional support staff.

A second challenge is the preparation and formation of retired public school administrators and teachers who are increasingly being appointed to leadership roles in Catholic schools, either as superintendents or principals. Unlike their public school counterparts, Catholic school superintendents and principals have to "do it all" often with little administrative and professional support staff. These otherwise qualified public school administrators often experience a culture shock when they move into positions of leadership in Catholic schools.

Identification

Where will the leaders of Catholic schools come from in the future? The best place to look for leaders of Catholic schools is within our schools—the teachers who show leadership potential.

The reason for the establishment in 1983 of the Association of Catholic Leadership Programs (ACLP) was to prepare teachers who had been identified as potential leaders for their leadership roles. The association now numbers over 30 Catholic colleges and universities across the country. A graduate of an ACLP member institution writes: "Administrators who are good Catholics don't automatically make good Catholic school administrators. I am glad I graduated from a Catholic school leadership program because it gave me the specialized vision and skill set that helps me be a more effective and confident Catholic school leader."

When good leadership is in place, schools thrive.

Catholic schools are fertile grounds for emerging leaders. Research has shown that Catholic school principals seek as prospective teachers, persons of deep faith, who are active in the Church, who would be good Christian role models, and who see teaching as a vocation or as a ministry. In the surveys of teachers that I have done as part of diocesan strategic planning studies, almost half of the teachers give a mission-related reason as their primary reason for teaching in the school.

Those who are identified for leadership positions need to have the "right stuff." Leaders of Catholic schools must possess the qualities outlined by Maria Ciriello in her three volume work: *The Principal as Educational Leader* (1993), *The Principal as Managerial Leader* (1994a), and *The Principal as Spiritual Leader* (1994b).

The research on effective schools emphasizes the importance of the principal as the instructional leader and shows that the principal's leadership has a positive influence on teachers' sense of efficacy. Effective Catholic schools must also have principals who exercise strong leadership in the creation of the school's faith community. Any school is challenged when it has a weak principal, a non-supportive pastor, and/or poor rapport between a pastor and a principal. Fortunately, the vast majority of Catholic schools are blessed with strong principals and supportive pastors. Examples of charismatic principals of Catholic schools abound. The National Catholic Educational Association continually seeks them out for recognition at its annual meeting.

Effective leaders exercise their educational leadership by setting goals that are consistent with the school's mission and by their ability to implement their vision for the school. Effective leaders are able to create an academic environment that reflects the school's Catholic identity and by cultivating the support of all stakeholders for these priorities. Carr's (1995) findings from a national study of 612 Catholic elementary school principals are consistent with the common understanding that leadership in Catholic schools is exercised in a particular mission context and is directed toward achieving both religious and academic goals. Both mission-related and professional reasons influenced the principals' reasons for remaining in a leadership position.

Preparation

How do we prepare leaders for Catholic schools? I will concentrate on the preparation of superintendents here. Ciriello's three facets of leadership expected of Catholic school principals provide a framework for the preparation of leaders. A Catholic school superintendent must be a person of faith with good administrative, management and interpersonal skills.

He or she must be knowledgeable about current educational trends and understand the need for and the value of strategic planning. In addition, a superintendent must understand and be comfortable in the context in which they will be working, especially those who work or aspire to work in diocesan central offices.

The Catholic Educational Leadership Program at The Catholic University of America is a research and practitioner oriented Ph.D. program designed to prepare superintendents of Catholic schools. The program is offered as a residential cohort model in four consecutive summers with some work carrying over via distance education into the fall and spring semesters. In addition to courses in research, evaluation, foundations, administration and leadership typically found in graduate leadership programs, the program includes units on building faith community, administering diocesan school systems, understanding diocesan administrative structures, religious education, history and mission of Catholic schools, Catholic school research, and contemporary issues in Catholic education.

Conclusion

Leadership is the key to the continuing success of Catholic schools. We must do everything in our power to identify, prepare and support qualified individuals for key leadership positions.

John Convey, Ph.D., is the St. Elizabeth Ann Seton Professor of Education at The Catholic University of America.

Carr, K. (1995). *Catholic elementary school leadership: A study of principals' motivation, efficacy and satisfaction.* Unpublished doctoral dissertation, The Catholic University of America, Washington, DC.

Ciriello, M. (1993). *The principal as educational leader: Expectations in the areas of leadership, curriculum, and instruction.* Washington, DC: United States Catholic Conference.

Ciriello, M. (1994a). *The principal as managerial leader: Expectations in the areas of personnel management, finance, and development.* Washington, DC: United States Catholic Conference.

Ciriello, M. (1994b). *The principal as spiritual leader: Expectations in the areas of faith development, building Christian community, moral and ethical development, history and philosophy.* Washington, DC: United States Catholic Conference.

Notre Dame Task Force on Catholic Education. (2006). *Making God known, loved, and served: The future of Catholic primary and secondary schools in America.* Notre Dame, IN: Author.

Presentation IV: Ronald Nuzzi

The formation of future leaders for service in education is a common theme in both the public and private sector. Educational research is clear regarding the leadership of the principal: it is the linchpin of overall school success (Marzano, 2003). With the dramatic changes that have transpired regarding the staffing of Catholic schools in the past four decades—namely, the shift from a predominantly religious and clerical faculty and administration to lay teachers and principals—the professional, academic preparation and spiritual formation of the faculty and administration are of particular importance.

What is new in the current situation is the emphasis on spiritual formation. In a previous generation, pastors, parents, diocesan officials, and universities did not concern themselves with the spiritual formation of Catholic school educators. Such formation was typically supplied via religious communities and congregations through their induction processes leading to religious profession or vows. Professional preparation programs today now face the relatively new reality of having to supply both coursework in the academic areas required as well as some basic religious education and catechesis. Time constraints and financial pressures also drive such programs because states have increasingly complex certification standards for teachers and principals, accountability is a legislative buzzword, and Catholic education professionals typically do not have the disposable income available to afford extensive graduate education.

Professional preparation programs today now face the relatively new reality of having to supply both coursework in the academic areas required as well as some basic religious education and catechesis.

A commonly researched theme surrounding the question of formation is the notion of Catholic identity. What are the constitutive elements of Catholic identity? What can, or should, be predicated of a Catholic school that is unique and not attributable to other educational environments, even private ones? Recent research has framed it thusly: What makes a Catholic school Catholic? The logic here is clear, if somewhat circular. Decide what constitutes a Catholic school—its distinguishing, unique characteristics. Then, hire for mission and recruit those teachers and administrators who can, by their lives and service, contribute to that identity.

While answers to the Catholic identity question are numerous (Groome, 1996; Nuzzi, 2001; Pilarczyk, 1996; Quirin, 2001), Catholicism as a lived experience and Catholic theology as an articulation of that experience are both essential to understanding what constitutes a Catholic institution. One would expect professional theologians to influence the shape of Catholic identity at the university level. However, Catholic educators in typical parish elementary schools and diocesan and private high schools are relatively unaccustomed to professional theological discourse in relation to the operation of K-12 education. This presents a challenge to preparation programs and church leaders, for theological convictions are at the heart of the identity question. Ellis Joseph, Dean Emeritus of the School of Education at the University of Dayton, wrote:

> *What makes Catholic schools Catholic are the theological truths which govern and give guidance to both philosophy and to persons of Catholic faith. These truths have made*

> *the Catholic church a countercultural church....The failure on the part of Catholic schools to understand that their guidance emanates from theology, and not solely philosophy, may account for their problems with identity and distinctiveness.* (Joseph, 2001, pp. 31-32)

Part of the formation of future teachers and leaders, it would seem, must include a strong formational component, fashioned on the core convictions of Catholicism.

This assertion is in no way intended to devalue teacher education or educational administration. Rather, it is acknowledging a staffing reality wherein our human resources no longer arrive to work with a high degree of theological literacy or personal faith formation. Preparation programs need not become seminaries or houses of religious formation, but they must certainly find ways to present respective disciplines from the viewpoint of a Catholic faith, eventually arriving, in both theory and practice, at an education that is uniquely Catholic. Moreover, this faith formation and personal appropriation of Catholic theological convictions are not extrinsic to the educator's professional preparation, nor should they be viewed as somehow compartmentalized and separate from developing a professional skill set and knowledge base. Indeed, this is precisely the flaw in the most popular articulation of the role of the Catholic school principal as involving three responsibilities: educational, managerial, and spiritual (Ciriello, 1993). Spiritual formation and leadership are not responsibilities one exercises in addition to educational and managerial responsibilities. Catholic identity requires that all educational and managerial activities be imbued with a spiritual disposition that contributes to establishing and strengthening the Catholic ethos of the school as well as the faith development of students and staff.

> *Part of the formation of future teachers and leaders, it would seem, must include a strong formational component, fashioned on the core convictions of Catholicism.*

The recruitment and formation of future teachers and leaders must take into consideration this need for coupling high quality professional preparation with an equally strong and rigorous approach to personal faith formation, education in the Catholic faith, and spiritual growth understood as a lifelong process. Openness to this theological education and faith formation ought to be considered as prerequisites for participation in preparation programs and sought after as much as academic credentials. Such an approach will help to shape educational institutions that are both truly Catholic and high quality schools. Allowing one or the other to take precedence will eventually result in an unbalanced situation, where a school and its faculty might have strong, academic standards but little regard for the Catholic faith, as a subject or a lifestyle. Or, alternatively, an exclusive emphasis on faith formation could result in a happy community of like-minded Catholics who are not engaged in any serious learning beyond their religious faith.

Ciriello, M. (1993). *The principal as educational leader: Expectations in the areas of leadership, curriculum, and instruction.* Washington, DC: United States Catholic Conference.

Groome, T. (1996). What makes a school Catholic? In T. McLaughlin, J. O'Keefe, & B. O'Keeffe (Eds.), *The contemporary Catholic school: Context, identity, and diversity* (pp. 107-125). London: Falmer.

Joseph E. (2001). The philosophy of Catholic education. In T. Hunt, E. Joseph, & R. Nuzzi (Eds.), *Handbook of research on Catholic education* (pp. 27-64). Westport, CT: Greenwood Press.

Marzano, R. J. (2003). *What works in schools: Translating research into action.* Alexandria, VA: Association for Supervision and Curriculum Development.

Nuzzi, R. (2002). Catholic identity. In T. Hunt, E. Joseph, & R. Nuzzi (Eds.), *Catholic schools still make a difference: Ten years of research 1991-2001* (pp. 9-20). Washington, DC: National Catholic Educational Association.

Pilarczyk, D. (1998). What is a Catholic school? *Origins, 28*(23), 405-408.

Quirin, L. (2001, February 9). What makes a school Catholic? *The Messenger*, (Suppl.), p. 1.

A Reflection by Patricia Helene Earl, I.H.M.

In reviewing the various presentations on the importance of strengthening the field of Catholic education and its development through three approaches, namely, forming teachers and leaders for Catholic schools, expanding and enhancing scholarship to improve the educational quality of Catholic schools, and ensuring the financial stability and accessibility of Catholic schools for students of today and tomorrow, I was delighted to see this conversation begin. Certainly, the financial stability and accessibility issue is a serious one. However, I would like to address the issue of forming teachers and leaders for Catholic schools by sharing the positive results of my research, thus somewhat combining the first two issues.

Having served as Assistant Superintendent of Schools for 13 years in the Diocese of Arlington (1990-2003), I became increasingly aware of the importance of forming teachers and leaders in our Catholic schools. I believe that teachers are the leaders of their classrooms much as various administrators are the leaders of the school. In focusing on the three areas of leadership that have been identified—educational, managerial, and spiritual (Ciriello, 1993, 1994a, 1994b)—I believe that there are many programs that help to develop the educational and managerial dimensions of leadership for both teachers and administrators. However, from my experience of interviewing hundreds of potential teachers, I know that the area of spiritual leadership is often the least understood and developed. I agree with Bishop Aymond that "As our teachers are formed in faith, or given the opportunity to be formed in faith, they will be able to hand on the faith to others." I believe that this needs to be a three-pronged process of information, formation, and transformation.

> *...from my experience of interviewing hundreds of potential teachers, I know that the area of spiritual leadership is often the least understood and developed.*

In 1997, I developed a series of seminars for the Diocese of Arlington in the area of virtue and in spirituality. In the virtue seminar (Earl, 2006), we basically spent two days teaching or reviewing concepts such as Baptism, grace, virtue, theological and moral virtues, conscience formation, moral development and leadership to both principals and teachers. In addition, while enriching the participants' knowledge or information on these topics, we offered numerous resources on how to make this come alive for students in the classroom. I also developed a four-week seminar on "Tips in Spirituality." This program focused on identifying what we mean by spirituality in the Christian or Catholic tradition while teaching some basic elements of prayer. Each week we focused on understanding and experiencing traditional prayers of the Church, the Liturgy of the Hours, the Mass, and Meditation. Throughout the classes, participants were awakened or reawakened to the importance of prayer in their own lives in order to develop a personal relationship with Christ as individuals and as members of the Church. They went through this process of information, formation, and transformation. In 2003, as I continued to offer these seminars, my study of the impact that these two programs had on the participants, their teaching pedagogy, and their understanding of the mission of the Church showed overwhelmingly positive results (Earl, 2003).

Based on the premise that you cannot give what you do not have, we gave the participants classroom activities to teach virtue and provide moral education for students. In addition, we gave them a renewed understanding so that they were enthused, revitalized and empowered to create virtue programs for their students not because it was someone's directive, but because they saw the meaning and value of promoting virtue in their schools. They were nourished by a few simple prayer experiences and wanted to continue to make time for their own personal prayer. Prayer time in school became vital and central to the mission of Catholic education. As a result of receiving the information in these seminars, the participants were being formed in the faith and transformed in their appreciation of developing a personal relationship with Christ. They were newly motivated to share this with their students and newly motivated in their understanding of the mission of Catholic education.

Based on my own research and program development (Earl, 2007), I am convinced that it is vitally important to form teachers and leaders not only in content area and best practices or principles of educational and managerial leadership, but also in their own faith formation. I believe that we need to open their eyes to the mission of Catholic education, which means helping them to recognize that if Christ and the faith formation of our students is the center of a Catholic school, then Christ and a vibrant faith must first be the center of their lives. Similar programs and continued research are essential.

Sister Patricia Helene Earl, I.H.M., Ph.D., is an Assistant Professor and Director of the Catholic School Leadership Program at Marymount University.

Ciriello, M. (1993). *The principal as educational leader: Expectations in the areas of leadership, curriculum, and instruction.* Washington, DC: United States Catholic Conference.

Ciriello, M. (1994a). *The principal as managerial leader: Expectations in the areas of personnel management, finance, and development.* Washington, DC: United States Catholic Conference.

Ciriello, M. (1994b). *The principal as spiritual leader: Expectations in the areas of faith development, building Christian community, moral and ethical development, history and philosophy.* Washington, DC: United States Catholic Conference.

Earl, P. (2003). *Formation of lay teachers in Catholic schools: The influence of virtues/spirituality seminars on lay teachers, character education and perceptions on Catholic Education.* Unpublished doctoral dissertation, George Mason University, Fairfax, VA.

Earl, P. (2006). *Building the builders: Faith formation in virtue.* Washington, DC: National Catholic Educational Association.

Earl, P. (2007). Challenges to faith formation in contemporary Catholic schooling in the USA: Problems and response. In G. Grace & J. O'Keefe (Eds.), *International handbook of Catholic education: Challenges for school systems in the 21st century* (pp. 37-60). New York: Springer.

A Reflection by Maureen Hackett

In a perfect world, Karen Ristau's notion that "those preparing for leadership positions would already be serving in Catholic education" would be a great answer to sustaining the legacy of strong Catholic leadership in our Catholic schools. Realistically, however, this is not an answer, and so we must address the need to attract talented leaders to our schools, as well as to provide these leaders with an opportunity for ongoing professional training and growth. More importantly, we must address the need to design a program to retain our talented leaders. How is it possible to compensate these faith-filled leaders without compromising the mission?

> *We need to hire not just great but, in fact, truly extraordinary principals.*

We need to hire not just great but truly extraordinary principals, charismatic, well-trained, knowledgeable leaders who, like any highly sought-after CEO in the business world, can have a deep impact upon the people they supervise as well as the organization they manage.

Leadership qualities differ from position to position. Key qualities necessary to be a successful Catholic school principal include strong management skills, deep faith and outstanding interpersonal skills. The day-to-day management of an educational institution requires clear vision, as well as strong organization, delegation, and communication skills in order that agendas, budgets and timelines are met. Principals need to have not only the ability to manage faculty and staff, but also the panache to work closely with parents, the school board and the funding partners to assure the vision and mission of the school.

I firmly believe that inspirational, CEO-like principals are the key to the renewal of Catholic education. Moreover, they could be instrumental in attracting new teachers and could serve as mentors to future principals and administrators in the educational pipeline. In having a positive reputation and, more importantly, in creating one for their school, excellent principals can attract new students from far and wide, as the principal is the face of the organization. Consequently, a successful principal should have the ability to attract good philanthropic partners, and must have the skills for fundraising as well as "friend" raising. In partnership with the school board, the principal supports the development activities managed by parents and board members. With the help of the endowment/foundation board, the principal's ability to clearly articulate the vision and mission of the school can have a profound effect on the future of the facilities, scholarships and perception held by the community at large.

Following the example of the business community, we need to offer attractive, competitive compensation to these would-be CEO's of our schools. If we do indeed hire leaders who are truly extraordinary, we owe it to these leaders to compensate them well for their work. In the situation where, as a result of the leadership skills of the principal, the revenue targets have been met or exceeded, the expenses controlled or reduced, the faculty and staff expectations fulfilled, and the support from the students and their families clearly expanded, it makes only good sense to create a plan for rewarding an outstanding performance.

One way to reward talented Catholic school leaders would be to provide them with opportunities for continued professional training and education. Another way is to set aside a "bonus" pool created with seed money from a foundation or financial gift. Additionally, I think giving our principals the opportunity to reward the exceptional performance of a faculty or staff member is something worth considering as well. Teachers are our schools' most valuable assets, and it is important to recognize these talented, faith-filled individuals. Finally, with the help of a human resources professional, a compensation package should be designed to not only attract talented leaders, but help to retain their talents and avoid their loss to public education.

In the words of John Convey, we need teachers and principals with the "right stuff." Now it's just up to us to do the "right thing" by hiring only the best so they can lead Catholic education into the bright future its history and heritage demands.

Maureen O'Gara Hackett's professional experiences include positions as Coordinator of Nursing Staffing at Evanston Hospital, Executive Assistant for the Dean of Organizational Behavior at Harvard Business School and as a Pharmaceutical Sales Representative with Riker Laboratories, Inc.

A Reflection by Rosemary Croghan

I am a lifelong supporter of Catholic education. Although I do not bring an academic's perspective to the conversation about Catholic schools, I have witnessed significant changes in Catholic education, from the early "golden" years when enrollment in schools was at its peak to today's troubling succession of school closings. The reasons for such changes have already been told. In reflecting on these issues, what is most disconcerting to me is that many of our remaining Catholic schools have drifted from the strong Catholic identity that once distinguished them from the public schools. Diocesan and national programs are addressing this identity problem in a variety of ways, but what new steps can be taken to enhance the Catholic culture of our schools? Hopefully, the conversation that began last September in Palo Alto will bring about lasting, positive changes. Thank you to Notre Dame and the Carnegie Foundation for initiating this conversation.

I cannot help but be optimistic when I witness these creative approaches to renewal and hope for the future of Catholic education.

As a trustee who is a member of the Catholic identity committees of two high schools and one university, I find myself asking several questions: What do we mean by "Catholic identity" or by "hire for mission?" Does the concept of Catholic identity differ from diocese to diocese or from school to school? How does one measure it? Certainly the issue becomes more complex when the student body of a Catholic school is predominantly non-Catholic. How do administrators establish Catholic identity in such a school? Do school boards make the preservation of Catholic identity a priority in their decision making?

The Carnegie Conversation panelists addressed many of these questions in their presentations. Fr. Ron Nuzzi in particular makes a strong argument for the formation and education of future school leaders as a critical step in renewing Catholic identity in schools. In my experiences of working with high school communities the relationship between Catholic identity and the formation of teachers is significant.

For example, the suburban Catholic high school I work with attracts the majority of its students from the surrounding K-8 parish schools. It has become apparent that the depth of knowledge and faith formation that incoming students receive in these schools varies widely. For the most part, the high school must fill in substantial gaps in students' knowledge of Catholic doctrine. On the other hand, the urban Catholic high school I am involved in accepts some 80% of its students from the local public schools, in keeping with its mission to serve the families who could not afford tuition at other Catholic schools. These students are culturally Catholic but unschooled in Catholic teaching, so faith instruction must start from the beginning.

Therefore, in spite of their differences, both schools have to deal with incoming classes whose knowledge of the Catholic faith is inconsistent and generally inadequate. It makes one question, especially in the case of the suburban school, the quality of the catechesis in our parish schools.

Of course it may be that the traditions of the faith, daily prayer, weekly Mass, and the receiving of the sacraments are not being passed on to children by their parents, thus placing a greater responsibility on schools.

Whatever the cause or causes may be, both schools are solving their problems of student formation through teacher formation. They recognize the truth in the words of Isocrates in *Antidosis*: "One who wishes to persuade others will not be negligent of his own virtue, but will pay special attention to it" (15:278). They are investing time and money into faith formation programs for faculty and staff, and implementing programs to educate parents and students alike, in hopes that they will actively participate in the Church.

These are examples of effective and encouraging steps that Catholic schools can take to secure their Catholic identity. I cannot help but be optimistic when I witness these creative approaches to renewal and hope for the future of Catholic education. I am equally inspired by all that is being done by our Catholic universities and by others who treasure Catholic education. I hope that the Carnegie workshop is only the beginning of great things to come. We owe it to our students, our parents, and our donors to provide the very best in Catholic education. We must collaborate to preserve our great educational tradition, rooted in Gospel values, for the sake of the Church and for the sake of all children, affluent or poor, who attend our schools.

Rosemary Croghan is a Gallagher Scholar Mentor, counseling promising students attending Chicago's Big Shoulders' schools. She is a Trustee of Loyola University and was a member of the founding Board of Trustees of Cristo Rey Jesuit High School.

A Reflection by John Croghan

I believe we have opportunities to reverse enrollment trends if we stress Catholic identity—that which makes our Catholic schools different—rather than just strive to imitate our richer public counterparts.

My response is prompted by Fr. Ronald Nuzzi's argument that the formation of Catholic principal leaders must include an emphasis on Catholic identity and that religious beliefs must be the core of this identity. His remarks resonate with me because I believe that in the long run, Catholic schools will be viable only if they maintain a strong Catholic identity, and if parents make this *raison d'etre* paramount in choosing a school for their children.

I am familiar with the different segments of the Catholic educational landscape in Chicago. In my suburban parish, where tuition would not be a serious obstacle for the generally affluent parents, they still elect by a 3 to 1 margin to send their children to the local public schools. The public schools are ranked among the best in the nation and parents want any educational edge that their real estate taxes can buy. It is not surprising that parents would not want to pay tuition at a Catholic school when there are attractive public alternatives. The parish school parents, however, believe that their school provides a comparable education. They tolerate an old building and fewer accoutrements only because they desire the Catholic ethos, but they are a static minority.

At the lowest end of the economic spectrum, parents of children in the poorest neighborhoods generally choose Catholic schools for their moral dimension but also because they perceive that the schools offer a safer environment and a better education than the local public schools. It has been a great work of the Archdiocese of Chicago to support these schools with their largely minority enrollments. Generous benefactors have provided the funds to keep them open and provide scholarships, because tuition is often not affordable. Hopefully, the inner-city public schools will improve, and then the Catholic schools would have to attract parents on the basis of the school's "core convictions," to use Nuzzi's words.

Maybe we will continue to see enrollment decrease to some smaller sustainable size. It may be that in a more assimilated American Catholic Church, within a more individualistic and relativistic society, this is the time to consider new models, especially for elementary schools. But I believe we have opportunities to reverse enrollment trends if we stress Catholic identity—that which makes our Catholic schools different—rather than just strive to imitate our richer public counterparts. I believe parents can be persuaded of the importance of faith-based education for their children in addition to academic excellence. The optimism and vitality of the Carnegie Conversation is a hopeful sign of the times.

John Croghan currently serves as Chairman and Managing Director of Rail-Splitter Capital Management, an investment firm in Chicago. John is also a trustee and serves on the investment committees of the Archdiocese of Chicago, Chicago Historical Society, Lyric Opera, Northwestern University and Big Shoulders Fund.

Strengthening and Applying
Scholarship
on Religious Character and
Academic Excellence

Presentation I: Daniel Lapsley

A field of study is marked by "disciplined inquiry" by a community of scholars into a shared problematic. A field of study begins with a problem, or set of related problems informed by theory, and is sustained by an infrastructure of professional conferences, organizations and journals. The field of moral education is used as one example of how this might work, along with recent work of the Center for Ethical Education in framing integrative research questions on a distinctive Catholic approach to moral character education. I conclude with suggestions for the next steps in building a field of Catholic education.

An Analogy: The Field of Moral Education

How do we develop scholars and foster more scholarship on Catholic and faith-based education? How might we enhance research and the application of research to improve the educational experience—assessment, curriculum, pedagogy, religious character—in Catholic and faith-based schools? One way to address these questions is to examine the formation of related fields of study, such as the field of moral education. In the 1960s there was no such field. At the time American psychology was largely in the grips of a behavioral paradigm that paid little attention to questions of values, moral development or education other than the application of the "laws of learning" to classrooms. But there was discernible movement among a younger generation of scholars to explore the implications of an emerging paradigm of cognitive development, better known in Europe but virtually absent from American departments of psychology. This paradigm was, of course, based on the writings and research of the great Swiss scholar, Jean Piaget.

A field of study begins with a problem, or set of related problems informed by theory, and is sustained by an infrastructure of professional conferences, organizations and journals.

Piaget was a self-styled "genetic epistemologist" whose life project was to ascertain criteria for judging progress in philosophy, mathematics and science. He attempted to discern such criteria by observing how children understood certain mathematical and scientific concepts; and by noting how this understanding was transformed with development. It was possible to show, for example, that the reasoning of later stages was more adaptive and powerful than the reasoning of earlier stages—and hence a developmental criterion was found to indicate progress and growth.

This perspective was highly attractive to a young clinical psychology graduate student at the University of Chicago. Larry Kohlberg came to his studies with a compelling question: How can the resources of psychology help provide the grounds for defeating ethical relativism? As he looked around psychology, he found that the two dominant paradigms viewed morality either as unconscious phenomena (psychoanalysis) or else as scientifically vapid unless operationally defined into terms (positive reinforcement) that gave comfort to relativism. But in Piaget's stage theory Kohlberg found what was wanted, which developmental criteria for ascertaining when certain moral positions were inadequate. Moreover, the model of deliberative reasoning as the highest stages showed the way to forge moral consensus.

For the next few decades Kohlberg and colleagues honed their assessment of moral reasoning and articulated a cognitive developmental approach to socialization that immediately held out implications for education. The stage theory and its model of growth suggested certain classroom strategies for advancing moral development, including dilemma discussion and democratic participation. Seminal papers appeared in scholarly edited volumes and journals. This attracted considerable interest among a small group of Kohlberg's students. A nascent Association for Moral Education (AME) was formed, with small meetings held around Boston, and then eventually at other universities. As interest grew, AME attracted other scholars so that, over the years, the association has become international, and represents more divergent and diverse perspectives on moral psychology, moral development and moral character education. AME has its own periodical, *Journal of Moral Education*, and numerous scholarly edited volumes have provided an outlet for scholarship. Moreover, opportunities for meetings, collaboration and conversation expanded to larger professional organizations, such as the American Educational Research Association (AERA), where moral education is planted as a Special Interest Group. The cumulative effect is that there is now a discernible field of moral education where none existed before.

Several lessons can be drawn from this example. The field of moral education emerged when a determined and charismatic scholar made innovative use of a rich theoretical tradition to take on a set of fundamental questions that go to the very heart of our moral life. Kohlberg's was a mind concentrated on an idea, and I think it was the very audacity of the idea, the urgency of the questions, and the powerful theoretical framework that made sense of it all, that dazzled a generation of young scholars to take up the plough in a fertile new field of discovery. I should add one more attraction, which was the prospect of applying the findings of this emergent field to the moral formation of children. The whole point of moral stage theory was to provide the conceptual grounding and pedagogy for changing the way we educate children—and this educational objective gave the field its ultimate purpose.

> *Like Kohlberg we must become, collectively, a mind concentrated on an idea.*

If the analogy to moral education is apt, then it points the way to a response to the questions put to the panel: How do we foster more scholarship on Catholic education? How do we enhance research and the application of research to improve the educational experience of children in Catholic and faith-based schools? The answer is threefold: First, we must articulate fundamental questions. Like Kohlberg we must become, collectively, a mind concentrated on an idea. Second, we must develop, or appropriate, powerful theoretical frameworks to address fundamental questions set before us. Third, we must see in our urgency to address theoretical problems the moral purpose of our inquiry.

I think the last two requirements are well in place. There does exist within the developmental and educational sciences powerful theoretical and empirical literatures to help us understand the dynamics of teaching and learning; what constitutes and how best to promote best practice instruction, curriculum development, effective school leadership, moral character formation, and more. What we know in the disciplines about learning and instruction, about effective curriculum, about school organization and leadership, applies just as well to children in Catholic schools, and their teachers, as in secular public schools. Moreover, the very fact of our gathering here attests to the sense of urgency we all feel in improving the lot of Catholic education in America. Theory and moral purpose we have in abundance. What we lack are fundamental questions worthy of the effort. What we lack are questions around which a field of study can coalesce.

Questions as Preliminary to a Field: ND Task Force

Insofar as problems and questions are preliminary to a field of inquiry, what questions should animate the emergent field of Catholic education? We know what good education looks like, but what constitutes good Catholic education?

What does "Catholic," used as an adjective, add to what we know about good education more generally? Perhaps more urgently, what is the "value proposition" that Catholic schools hold out to parents and stakeholders?

In their Final Report, *Making God Known, Loved, and Served: The Future of Catholic Primary and Secondary Schools in the United States*, the Notre Dame Task Force on Catholic Education (2006) urges the building of a "field of Catholic education" through studying how child development is nurtured in a "climate where faith is taken seriously," (p. 9).

Here is a good start in framing the questions preliminary to a field. How is child development nurtured in a climate of faith? Put differently, the Task Force appears to ask how it is possible to integrate the scholarly literatures of child development with the "climate of faith" of the Catholic tradition. How is it possible, in other words, to integrate the resources of the Catholic tradition—its metaphors, images and claims—with the theories, constructs and findings of the developmental and educational sciences to improve the lot of children, to enhance their moral formation, to equip them for the demands of responsible citizenship. In my view this is the dazzling "big idea" that makes common cause and shared agendas worthwhile; that attracts a younger generation of scholars to plough the field. In short, the field of Catholic education will be found at the crossroad of the Catholic tradition and the developmental and educational sciences.

An Example from the Center for Ethical Education (CEE)

I would offer the work of the Notre Dame Center for Ethical Education as an example of how a research agenda might get launched. Our deliberation began with a set of related questions. What would instructional practice look like if it was guided by the Catholic Catechism? Does the lived experience of the Christian faith, as articulated in Scripture and Catholic tradition, suggest a range of pedagogies appropriate for distinctly Catholic education? And would the distinctly Catholic pedagogy align with professionally responsible instructional practices as underwritten by the knowledge base of developmental and educational science?

The religious identity of Catholic is distinguished in our view by its vision of faith community as the basis of learning and by its Trinitarian understanding of the relational basis of personal identity. Moreover, the Catholic tradition holds out a suite of regulative concepts that articulate what the life of Christian virtue might look like, concepts such as sacrament, vocation, forgiveness, beatitudes, and agape, among others. Indeed, the Catholic identity of schools, in our view, is marked by classroom experiences that are Trinitarian, agapic, sacramental, vocational, communal, and beatific.

But this explicitly religious framework finds resonance in scholarly research on the importance of school climate, the sense of community and other relational, affective features of the school experience. For example, the Trinitarian conception of God and the nature of church provide robust metaphors of community that align with psychological literatures on communal classroom and school organization. It aligns with scholarly literatures on the importance of caring classrooms, school bonding and attachment to teacher, classroom and school community.

What's more, an education rigorously grounded on the core assumptions of the Christian faith also presents counter cultural visions of how we are to relate to each other and to the community, how we approach failure, of what matters in discipline, and more. Hence the convergence of Catholic tradition and developmental science is not simply a religious gloss on what is known better by the scholarly academic literatures, but rather the religious dimension is a challenge to it. Research on Catholic education is ideally prophetic in the sense that it contributes unique perspectives on the mechanisms of effective education more generally. It serves a broad public purpose insofar as it generates models of effective educational innovation and prepares Catholic and non-Catholic students for living well the life of Christian vocation and service.

Of course, the rich concepts of the Catholic tradition are theological, transcendent, articles of faith, and are always under determined by the tools of reason. Yet the Catholic commitment to the sacramental principle gives us confidence that richly theological concepts must live and breathe and do their work in the daily experiences of Christian life, including the experiences of children in classrooms and schools.

> *The Catholic identity of schools, in our view, is marked by classroom experiences that are Trinitarian, agapic, sacramental, vocational, communal, and beatific.*

That said, instructional practice and educational leadership that is animated by distinctly Catholic concepts (e.g., vocation, community, sacrament, the beatitudes, agape, forgiveness, and so on) is still an evolving challenge set before the emerging field of Catholic education. Yet we are confident school practices that support caring classroom communities will provide the starting point for reflection on a distinctive Catholic pedagogy.

Next Steps

A field of study requires more than an animating idea. Hard questions, strong theory, a motivating purpose, these are the first steps. But if moral education is any guide, the field of Catholic education requires professional structures to provide opportunities for researchers to share their work, to collaborate and develop a communal sense of shared mission and common cause. The field of Catholic education also requires foundation support. Kohlberg's work at Harvard would not have been launched without the support of the Kennedy and Ford Foundations.

As shared collaborative research accumulates it may become necessary to form a new professional organization of Catholic education researchers (Association for Catholic Education Research-ACER) that would meet annually at various Catholic universities on a rotating basis.

But this is not the only place for Catholic education research to be discussed and promoted. Ultimately, the field of Catholic education should not serve narrow sectarian interests but speak to the common good of the educational sciences more broadly conceived. Models of Catholic school organization and practice, the proliferation of ways of instantiating the Catholic tradition as reflected in various conceptual frameworks, and research on these matters, will be a prophetic voice to the education community more generally. Forming a Special Interest Group (SIG) at the American Educational Research Association might be a way to speak to the broader educational science community.

Part of the discussion that takes place in these venues must surely focus on establishing a mechanism or opportunities for researchers across various Catholic universities and colleges to collaborate on common projects; and to establish a common data base that can be accessed by interested scholars. As any pastor will attest, the sense of community—or of field—emerges as an outcome of common effort for a common goal. A field of study is a dependent variable that results from disciplined inquiry into a shared problematic.

Moreover, fields of study gain legitimacy to the extent that they conform to standard notions of academic credibility, including formal structures that encourage engagement, criticism, peer review and publication. The most secure form of academic credibility is when a knowledge field is organized as an academic unit, or a professional body.

Consequently, new scholarly journals should be formed that focus on theoretical and empirical research and which engage the broader academic communities in the developmental and educational sciences, including sociology and allied empirical sciences. There is, of course, an extant journal of Catholic education that meets the need for historical, theological and philosophical analysis of Catholic education. I will note in passing that the field of music education has no less than six journals. The field of adolescent development has at least that many. In addition to new periodicals, we should pursue scholarly edited volumes that are not driven by advocacy but rather engagement with the larger educational science community.

> *Ultimately, the field of Catholic education should not serve narrow sectarian interests but speak to the common good of the educational sciences more broadly conceived.*

Admittedly, these professional structures are long-range markers that a field of Catholic education has emerged. Getting there will require hard questions, strong theory, mechanisms that support collaborative research, reliable sources of funding, and multiple outlets for scholarly publication that insist on the highest standards of peer review. Only when we make progress in addressing the value proposition with empirical data will a field of Catholic education come into better view.

Daniel Lapsley, Ph.D., is a Professor of Psychology at the University of Notre Dame.

Notre Dame Task Force on Catholic Education. (2006). *Making God known, loved, and served: The future of Catholic primary and secondary schools in America*. Notre Dame, IN: Author.

Presentation II: Joseph O'Keefe, S.J.

When I was at Radbaud University in Nijmegen, Netherlands, at a conference several years ago, I became familiar with a journal published by Brill Academic Publishers entitled, *The Journal of Empirical Theology*. As one who lives the U.S. academic context, I thought to myself, "Empirical theology...now there's an oxymoron." Though the notion of empirical theology may indeed be oxymoronic, the term expresses what I believe to be an important cornerstone of our efforts to define and nurture a field of Catholic education. How do we establish a field that weds the empirical wisdom of the social scientist and the contextual wisdom of the theologian with the practical wisdom of the practitioner?

The Empirical Wisdom of the Social Scientist

It is a lamentable fact that many in the Catholic education community have a disregard for research. Though the theory-practice divide is not unique to Catholic education, it is exacerbated by a number of factors. First, high-quality research is expensive and has often been beyond the capacity of the Catholic community. Second, while one of the great strengths of Catholic schools is their autonomy, it is also their great weakness; large-scale collaborative efforts at uniform data collection and analysis have been rare. Third, the Catholic community is still somewhat haunted by an anti-intellectualism that undervalues data-driven analysis and decision making. If we already possess "The Truth," why spend time and effort doing research to inform policy and practice? We need a concerted effort to instill a desire in every sector of the Catholic community to strengthen and apply scholarship on religious character and academic excellence. In the meantime, we can take some concrete steps.

We need a concerted effort to instill a desire in every sector of the Catholic community to strengthen and apply scholarship on religious character and academic excellence.

The U.S. Department of Education has been a major source of data about Catholic schools. For example, analysis of the High School and Beyond Study led James Coleman (1982) to put forward a "Catholic school effect" that can be explained by a high level of social capital. Other federal studies, including the National Assessment of Educational Progress (NAEP), the Educational Longitudinal Study (ELS), the National Household Education Survey (NHES), the School and Staffing Survey (SASS), and Private School Survey (PSS), are relevant to the field of Catholic education. One of our tasks is to influence topics and sampling frames to yield relevant information about academic excellence, such as comparable assessments of student learning across school sectors, long-term studies of educational attainment, studies of teacher quality, recruitment and retention and while less evident, some measures of religious character, such as student attitudes about civic engagement, service learning, parental attitudes. We also need to make concerted and collaborative efforts to prepare and support researchers who can mine these rich sources of data.

Federal data sets are not enough. We need to influence topics and procedures for standardized annual data collection across dioceses. Currently dioceses have a variety of methods of data collection and provide only aggregate data to the National Catholic Educational Association. This would be a relatively easy problem to resolve, given the possibilities provided by web-based technology. We also need to foster and coordinate sporadic surveys about pressing issues across sectors, national and regional, diocesan and religious-community sponsored. For example, a broader constituency could participate in the Student Profile Survey, a self-report instrument designed by the Jesuit Secondary Education Association to measure student attitude-belief and expectation-performance change from freshman to senior year in the five dimensions of the Profile of the Graduate of a Jesuit High School at Graduation: Open to growth, intellectually competent, religious, loving, and committed to doing justice. In an increasingly globalized world and as members of a worldwide church, we must also foster international comparative studies on the over 100,000 Catholic schools across the globe (Grace & O'Keefe, 2007) to shed new light on issues of academic performance and religious vitality.

Complex questions can rarely be answered by one method of inquiry. Though rigorous qualitative research is time-consuming and expensive, the breadth of large-scale studies are best complemented by the depth of case studies, which provide a richer picture of the issue under consideration and offer insights into the perspective of people on the ground. Such analyses are particularly helpful in efforts to understand the complexities of religious character.

The Contextual Wisdom of the Theologian

Catholic schools have a unique mission and culture. While they share the mission of any school—academic excellence, formation of character, the inculcation of civic engagement—they are charged with passing on religious faith to the next generation. Catholic schools provide a Catholic education for Catholic children, as mandated by the Third Plenary Council of Baltimore (1884). Though circumstances have changed dramatically in the past 123 years, the dual goals of religious literacy/practice, the understanding of and full participation in Roman Catholicism, and spiritual development, the desire for and experience of knowing God, remain. Increasingly in the USA, and for many years in non-Christian countries, Catholic schools have also provided a Catholic education for all children; the goal is not so much to provide an education for Catholic children, but to provide a Catholic education for anyone. Respectful of the religious background that non-Catholic students bring, the school encourages spiritual and moral development based on a Catholic philosophy (O'Keefe, 1999) that is accessible and meaningful to a broad audience. Whether the schools serves Catholic or non-Catholic children, they have a culture unlike any other school.

Without the active engagement of administrators, teachers, parents and students themselves, the emerging field of Catholic education, even with the rigor of social science and the depth of theologians, would be distorted and irrelevant.

Like their counterparts in every sector, Catholic educators need to be informed by the precision of the social scientists. Unlike their counterparts, they also need to be informed by scholars who have a deep understanding of the particular ecclesial context, the history and living tradition that permeates the culture of Catholic schools. A field of Catholic education requires that the work of social scientists be complemented by the work of theologians, philosophers and historians, the ones who bring contextual wisdom to this enterprise. In concert, these scholars can determine the questions that need to be addressed, and they can also bring a depth of insight to the analysis of data.

The Practical Wisdom of the Practitioner

Many at this gathering, Lee Shulman chief among them, have devoted much time and attention to the interplay between theory and practice in the world of education. In Catholic education, sadly, the chasm between theory and practice has been wide and deep. Without the active engagement of administrators, teachers, parents and students themselves, the emerging field of Catholic education, even with the rigor of social science and the depth of theologians, would be distorted and irrelevant. Conversely, without the empirical and contextual wisdom I have described above, the emerging field of Catholic education would continue to suffer the ill effects that we see today: timidity and fatigue in the face of change, perpetuation of the status quo, lack of engagement with the wider education world, and a fragmentation that leads to a constant reinvention of the wheel. Given chronic understaffing and financial constraints, it is far too often the case that the urgent overshadows the important.

It is incumbent upon us to create new structures that will focus attention on what is most important in Catholic education. One possible model is the Collaborative Fellows Program, which was designed to bridge the gap between researchers at Boston College and practitioners in the Boston Public Schools. Whatever the structure, the emerging field of Catholic education will depend upon the collaboration of scholars and practitioners to devise research questions, to collect data, to conduct analyses and, most importantly, to disseminate findings that will enhance practice.

[Rev. Joseph O'Keefe, S.J., Ed.D., is Dean of the Lynch School of Education at Boston College.

Coleman, J., Hoffer, T., & Kilgore, S. (1982). *High school achievement: Public, Catholic and private school compared.* New York: Basic Books.
Grace, G., & O'Keefe, J. (2007). *International handbook of Catholic education: Challenges for school systems in the 21st century.* New York: Springer
O'Keefe, L. (1999). Visionary leadership in Catholic schools. In J. Conroy (Ed.), *Inside out: Perspectives on Catholic education* (pp. 15-38). Dublin: Veritas.

Presentation III: Lorraine Ozar

Let me begin by providing a brief context for my remarks. Over the last two decades, I have worked with hundreds of Catholic schools and thousands of Catholic school educators in over 60 dioceses across the United States. My professional development work with Catholic schools in curriculum, assessment, and instructional leadership has spanned my career as a high school teacher and administrator, a professional member of the Office of Catholic Schools in the Archdiocese of Chicago, and currently as a faculty member and director of the Center for Catholic School Effectiveness in the School of Education at Loyola University Chicago. My perspective on building a field of Catholic education, expanding and enhancing scholarship to strengthen excellence, focuses on the unique bridging that Catholic universities can and must do between research and the lived experience of Catholic schools today.

And in all our work, we must demand of ourselves and the schools we serve that we insist on quality.

Catholic schools enjoy a long-standing reputation for providing solid academic preparation for students. During the "relevance" years of the 1970s, when many public schools and school systems were experimenting with individually guided instruction, alternative courses of study based on student choice, fewer requirements and more electives, Catholic schools for the most part stayed with the so-called "basics"—a core, required curriculum for all students grounded in language arts, mathematics, social studies, science, and religion. This allowed Catholic school students from all socioeconomic backgrounds to do pretty well in comparison to many public school counterparts in demonstrating fundamental learning skills. Of course, many Catholic schools did far more than this, but most did well enough to reinforce the assumption that academic excellence is a given in Catholic schools.

I believe that one of the greatest challenges now facing Catholic schools is overcoming a kind of inertia that has resulted from taking academic excellence for granted in many instances.

This is changing. As 21st century learning needs accelerate, as competition for students reaches acute levels, as legitimate demand for demonstrated results increases, many schools and dioceses are responding to the urgency of deliberate and transparent excellence. They need help. The Center for Catholic School Effectiveness (CCSE) was founded in 2003 precisely to respond to the critical need Catholic schools have for quality, research-based, on-going professional development that will enhance their capacity to strengthen their educational experience in curriculum, assessment, pedagogy, and religious character. Professional development that is provided by experts who also understand and embrace the mission and uniqueness of faith-based schools.

It is critical that this professional development be research-based. Schools have limited resources; students have limited time; the stakes are extremely high. We have to find out what works and then make it available to everyone. Michael Fullan and colleagues (2006) in the book, *Breakthrough*, refer to the moral imperative of education for our times as "raising the bar and closing the gap." This has always been at the heart of Catholic school mission. It is why Catholic schools often continue to provide the last, best hope for a better future for children in many inner-city communities.

In order to raise the bar and close the gap, Fullan suggests that we need to pay attention to the "3 Ps": personalization, precision, and professional learning. In other words, to seriously raise the bar and close the gap, we need to find ways of meeting each student's learning needs (personalization), using effectively targeted strategies that actually work (precision), delivered by teachers working in continuous improvement collaborative models (professional learning communities).

This is the research that needs doing in Catholic schools: how do Catholic educators working within the unique structures and context of Catholic school values and culture personalize learning for wider and wider bands of learners, make it more precise, and create new knowledge among teachers and administrators that readily informs everyone's decisions to improve teaching and learning. This is the research that needs doing in Catholic schools so that those who support Catholic educators through professional development and course work have a strong basis on which to design and implement interventions, training programs, and site-based coaching. We, here, and our many colleagues not here but with us in commitment to this work, need to find ways to support this research.

Building a field of Catholic education as we are discussing in these meetings, requires that there be a community of inquirers who have access to vehicles for sharing ideas, replicating studies, validating results, and disseminating findings. What can help? I will suggest three things for our conversation:

One, establish and support centers like CCSE and others around the country—the Center for Catholic Education at Boston College, the Institute for Catholic Educational Leadership at USF, the LEAD Center at Loyola Marymount, the Murray Institute at the University of St. Thomas, the Institute for Educational Initiatives at the University of Notre Dame—to name a few. Centers that focus on Catholic education within schools of education and other university units provide a designated and funded locus for faculty who want to engage in research in Catholic schools—a locus that can make it easier for universities to recruit and hire new faculty with interest in Catholic education research, easier to seek grants, easier to provide colleagues in the endeavor.

Two, recognize and support refereed journals like *Catholic Education: A Journal of Inquiry and Practice* and university presses like the newly established ACE Press at Notre Dame. Would-be-scholars need critical outlets for publications in a field of Catholic education. Without recognized and respected means for publication, non-tenured faculty will continue to have conflicting interests about engaging in Catholic education research.

Three, create regular forums for scholars in Catholic education to engage in debate and share research and ideas. There is an American Philosophical Association and an American Catholic Philosophical Association. There is an American Educational Research Association. Why not an American Catholic Educational Research Association?

Finally, the research can and should take many forms:

- Research that replicates studies done originally in the public sector, using subject populations entirely within Catholic schools to determine whether initial findings based on public school experience hold true in Catholic schools, or whether and how the unique elements of Catholic schools affect the results. For example, the research on "high yield" instructional strategies; or the recent Pianta classroom study.
- Research carried out directly in Catholic schools to identify and validate best practices within the unique Catholic school context. For example, effective strategies for developing Teacher Assistance Teams in Catholic elementary schools.

- Research focused on generating new knowledge in relation to religious character and faith formation, and the impact of faith consciousness on teaching and learning in the various disciplines. For example, research on the effectiveness of using the IPP—Ignatian Pedagogical Paradigm of experience, reflection, action—in Jesuit high schools.
- Longitudinal studies that tell the story of how students derive spiritual benefit from being in Catholic schools: effectiveness of catechesis, of formation programs, of enculturation factors.

And in all our work, we must demand of ourselves and the schools we serve that we insist on quality—quality defined as using evidence-based practices and demonstration of performance-based outcomes.

We have much work to do in the field of Catholic education and it can be done only if we bring our collaborative resources to bear on the issues. Following the principles of backward design curriculum planning, I would like to suggest that we collectively ask and answer three questions:

1. What are the characteristics of effective Catholic schools?
2. What constitutes good evidence of these characteristics?
3. What national "menu" of knowledge and training can we offer?

I believe that a truly collaborative response to these questions—each one supported by research—would infuse Catholic education with hope and energy supported and justified by a coherent plan for realizing results. On the way to developing a field of Catholic education, we might actually become a community of learners ourselves: taking individual responsibility, based on collective expectations, resulting in shared accountability for the future of Catholic education.

[Lorraine Ozar, Ph.D., is Director of the Center for Catholic School Effectiveness at Loyola University Chicago.

Fullan, M., Hill, P., & Crevola, C. (2006). *Breakthrough*. Thousand Oaks, CA: Sage.

Presentation IV: Mary Elizabeth Galt, B.V.M.

The two questions posed for today's panel, which I will address as a practitioner who has served as a teacher, principal, school supervisor, assistant superintendent and superintendent, are:

1. What happens in a faith-based educational institution?
2. How do I see the role of higher education impacting Catholic education?

Defining Faith-Based Education

The alignment of beliefs, values and traditions form the core of faith-based educational institutions.

What does faith-based education look like? What does it feel like? We all know when something feels just right. It can be said about a restaurant, a home, a person; the total package is "in sync." I can best explain it with the analogy of a restaurant. The décor, the cuisine, the staff all fit to create a feeling of completeness.

This is how I would describe a faith-based educational institution: Everything in the institution is aligned. There is a cohesiveness that is tangible to an outsider.

There are 274 schools in the Archdiocese of Los Angeles, and I have spent many hours in these schools. They span the gamut—rich, poor, middle-income, Caucasian, Hispanic, Asian, small, large, urban, suburban, even rural. The archdiocese extends over three counties—Los Angeles, Ventura and Santa Barbara—and some of our schools are in farming communities.

What are the common elements that make for this cohesiveness, for this focused environment? I would posit it is an institution with a firmly established philosophy, based on solid faith or a belief system.

It is certainly not difficult to define Catholic education as faith-based. Faith is of the very essence and the justification for our schools. For my purpose today, I will describe faith as a code of beliefs, a commitment to common values that flow from these beliefs and are lived out in traditions.

The alignment of beliefs, values and traditions form the core of faith-based educational institutions. From these flow the school's philosophy, mission statement, and vision statement, all of which anchor all that takes place in the school, what I would call the curriculum—using this in the broadest terms—everything that takes place in the school. Let me illustrate. I randomly selected this mission statement from one of our schools:

> Notre Dame Elementary School, in the tradition of the Sisters of Notre Dame, is committed to providing a thoroughly Catholic education in an academically challenging environment designed to nurture socially responsible citizens.

This mission statement links the
- Traditions of the Notre Dame Sisters to
- A thoroughly Catholic education—its beliefs—to
- The values of academic excellence and social responsibility.

If we were to line up all 274 school mission statements, these essential elements would be articulated.

Behind this one-sentence mission statement are the values inherent in practices that define faith-based education, some of which I highlight below as essential ingredients that, blended together, personify a faith-based school.

Our Catholic school leaders need to be reflective, intentional leaders.

- First, the value of belonging—a Catholic school is a place where a true sense of belonging is present. Each child is part of a family, a community—a huge, messy family that stretches over 2,000 years.

- Second, the value of being chosen—every child has a status, a place in the school, a sense of "they want me" that students come to trust. Because the student is selected, he or she has an importance and a value in the institution.

- Third, expectation—with this selection comes expectations of behavior, dress, attitude and consequences. Intrinsic to clearly articulated expectation is the building of character. Students taking responsibility for their behavior, knowing that their actions have not only an impact on them but on others—their classmates, their teachers, their parents, the school community.

- Fourth, the value of learning—the purpose of the faith-based school is to learn. This is an overt expectation. We cannot assume that children realize this, nor do their parents. Learning is a value the school must articulate in a very conscious, organized way. The environment, the discipline, the stance of the staff, the leadership must directly reinforce this focus. Coupled with the clearly-defined purpose—"we are here to learn"—is a commitment to be a lifelong learner.

- Fifth, control of the curriculum—unlike our colleagues in public education, our Catholic schools are free from the whims of politics to respond to the latest "fad" in education. Certainly, we must always look to the best of the new, while holding on to the best of the old, but this control over curriculum is critical to maintaining a faith-based school. We must remain above the pressures of special interest groups that want to influence and demand curriculum requirements.

- Sixth, the value of partnering with parents—the school, now more than ever, is an extension of the family. The strength of our Catholic schools has always been a close partnership with parents. This is the advantage of a small faith-based school. Parents are a vital presence in the life of the school. Andrew Greeley, in his research many years ago, identified this parent-school relationship as a key factor in the success of our Catholic schools. Parents pay tuition; therefore, they have invested in their child's education. Teachers and administrators realize the sacrifice parents are making and, in turn, have a commitment to educate their children. Parents realize teachers are making a sacrifice to teach in a Catholic school with less salary than their public colleagues, therefore, they support the teachers. We have a circle of support. The entire school community benefits from this intermingling of support, commitment and investment.

- Finally, number seven, the value of service to the community—a faith-based institution is training young people to see the needs of the less fortunate in our global village, to become responsible citizens in our world. This is integral to a faith-based school.

The Role of Higher Education

How can and should Catholic higher education positively impact Catholic education?

• Due to the decentralized governance of Catholic schools, the training and mentoring of present and future leaders is critical to our survival.

• Besides the traditional training in all our foundational Church documents on Catholic education, and the standard curriculum for the preparation of school leaders, our leaders today must be grounded in ethical behavior. We are seeing an increase in many unethical practices creeping into our schools: embezzlement, issues with our sports programs and boundary violations to name some of the most damaging. This may be the greatest crisis we face and has the potential to force some schools to close their doors.

• Higher education needs to provide our leaders with the skills to reflect on all their practices—finances, human resources, student achievement. Are all school practices fair, just and ethical? I see this as one of the greatest needs, and our Catholic school leaders need to be reflective, intentional leaders.

Sister Mary Elizabeth Galt, B.V.M. is Chancellor of the Archdiocese of Los Angeles.

A Reflection by Karen Ristau

The challenge in considering Catholic education as a field of study is to make this idea a reality: to establish a place for Catholic education in the academy as a legitimate endeavor. Lee Shulman in his keynote address suggests several reasons for establishing such a field of study, and Maureen Hallinan extended the clarification of a field as opposed to an academic discipline. I would add the importance of legitimacy and institutional presence to the conversation.

At the present time, some Catholic colleges and universities offer programs intentionally designed to prepare teachers for the Catholic school classroom as well as provide administrative knowledge and skills for those who are already or will be school leaders. These institutions of higher education, some of which are operating with limited resources and nominal support, have invented a variety of ways to provide this kind of vocational preparation. Creative and innovative financial models allow student participation at modest or no cost. The programs culminate in degrees, certificates or licensure. Practitioners, regular academic faculty or adjuncts, summer visitors and other people who have knowledge and experience in Catholic education teach courses. Service to Catholic school teachers and leaders is provided by departments, institutes, centers and other arrangements inside or along side the standard way of organizing a college or university. However, to my knowledge, no Catholic college or university has a named professor of Catholic education in a regular and recognized academic department whose work is aimed solely at teaching, scholarship and service in the field of Catholic education. That is precisely what is missing from promoting this splendid idea and validating this area of work for our Church as a sound and worthy endeavor.

> *Establishing Catholic education as a field of study requires the appointment of a person or persons whose academic work would be grounded in teaching and research about Catholic education.*

Establishing Catholic education as a field of study requires the appointment of a person or persons whose academic work would be grounded in teaching and research about Catholic education. Appointment and title is the usual way within the academy to formalize expectations and provide institutional presence. The way professors think of and name themselves—"I am a...."—influences the way they conduct themselves and how they are considered by others. The absence of those who are Catholic education professors by title unwittingly promotes role ambiguity and a certain invisibility. To establish positions named Professor of Catholic Education would, in effect, institutionalize the role which at present is more or less an informal one, and would add both credibility and visibility. Furthermore, it would raise the enterprise to a place of deserved prominence.

Shulman challenges Catholic higher education to establish a field of Catholic education, one which "will be vigorously, self-consciously and outrageously interdisciplinary" in order to accomplish what Hallinan describes as a work which has a "far more radical and challenging goal than simply to teach religion to students. It focuses on the fullness of Catholic life as taught and practiced in Catholic schools." In order to create such a field of study, there must be faculty named in the same way other faculty are named, appointed to full-time positions, conducting scholarship, service and research in Catholic education, whose institutional presence becomes a legitimate part of the university—and in more than one college or university. To do less will not result in the promise that Catholic education holds for the people of God.

A Reflection by Timothy Cook

I am grateful for the opportunity to respond to the Carnegie Conversation panelists. I found their remarks invigorating and thought-provoking. My remarks will focus on four issues: Placing priority on religious vitality research questions, expanding the international perspective, transforming university culture, and building research capacity.

Dan Lapsley contends that a field of study requires fundamental questions worthy of research. I enthusiastically endorse the position shared by all three panelists that we must frame questions about the religious identity of Catholic schools and address them empirically. Furthermore, in this age of assessment, accountability, and rising costs, we need to produce research that addresses foundational questions related to student and graduate religious outcomes such as: What are the measures of religious mission effectiveness? Are Catholic schools effective in their religious mission? Are Catholic school graduates distinctive? How is the Catholic school student experience different? These questions precede and complement questions offered by Lorraine Ozar that deal with the characteristics of effective Catholic schools and evidence thereof.

Recent research results about the Catholic school effect on religiosity in America are inconsistent and inconclusive. Some studies show few or small effects. To me, the biggest concern is not that recent research results are underwhelming in support of the Catholic school effect on religious outcomes. I am more alarmed by the small amount of research being done despite longstanding recommendations to make this a research priority (Convey, 1992; Hunt, Joseph & Nuzzi, 2002). Research, empirical and otherwise, about religious mission effectiveness is fundamental to the contribution and vitality of the Catholic school enterprise, and therefore it must be a priority.

Because Catholic schools are a worldwide phenomenon, we must be intentional about fostering an international perspective in our research, as Fr. Joseph O'Keefe suggests. For example, we should resist using "American" in the title of a new research organization. I know firsthand that we can learn much from Catholic educators and scholars in other countries. Most of my epiphanies have occurred in an international context. I attended the conference in The Netherlands that O'Keefe mentioned in his opening remarks. Australia serves as an awesome example of a country where Catholic schools are thriving and where a culture of collaborative research among scholars and practitioners already exists. Australian Catholic University's biennial International Conference on Catholic Educational Leadership provides us with a model of how to foster a culture of research among practitioners, focus on pertinent issues for faith schools, and spotlight the international character of Catholic education. To the best of my knowledge, nothing comparable exists in the United States. As a starting point, I would like to see us build bridges with Catholic educators and scholars in neighboring Canada and Mexico.

We need to reclaim Catholic education as a mission-centered priority.

To move forward, there are aspects of Catholic university culture that need to be confronted and transformed. The fact that Catholic universities no longer produce the majority of doctoral dissertations about Catholic education implies that Catholic education is a stepchild in our own institutions. We need to reclaim Catholic education as a mission-centered priority. Also, research in Catholic education is sometimes viewed as too narrow a focus that does not fit well in any discipline. In America, research about religious character and mission effectiveness of Catholic schools is especially problematic because it transcends the fields of religious education, theology, and organizational culture. Furthermore, as Bishop Aymond points out, we are very competitive. We expend too much energy fighting for preeminence, branding our initiatives, and building empires. As Karen Ristau likes to say, "There's plenty of work to go around." Moving forward, each institution's fundamental guiding questions should be: 1) What resources are we devoting to scholarship about Catholic schools and 2) What structures are we putting in place to facilitate conversation and collaboration within our institution, with other Catholic universities, and beyond?

The preceding questions center on building our research capacity to grow Catholic education into what Lee Shulman calls a "robust field." Among the panelist suggestions, I find two particularly compelling. First, establishing and endowing university centers and institutes to serve as the loci for interdisciplinary and collaborative Catholic school research is a strategy that offers tremendous promise. Second, creating a national or international organization that serves as a hub for Catholic school research has terrific merit. However, let's study this proposal as part of a grander design. In other words, perhaps it is time to create a super organization as a funded university network umbrella with designated personnel that houses a new research organization, as well as other existing university networks such as the Association of Catholic Leadership Programs (ACLP) and the University Consortium for Catholic Education (UCCE).

Timothy Cook, Ph.D., serves as Director of Secondary Education at Creighton University.

Convey, J. (1992). *Catholic schools make a difference: Twenty-five years of research*. Washington, DC: National Catholic Educational Association.
Hunt, T., Joseph, E., & Nuzzi, R. (2002). *Catholic schools still make a difference: Ten years of research 1991-2000*. Washington, DC: National Catholic Educational Association.

A Reflection by Gerald Cattaro

By commenting on the Supreme Court decision in *Zelman v. Simmons Harris* of June 27, 2002, the *New York Times* editorial ("The Wrong Ruling," 2002) may have paradoxically set the stage for Catholic educational as a field of study. In the editorial the *New York Times* made reference to Catholic schools in particular and their sacred fundamentals such as Mass, the Gospel and crucifixes. In addition it made reference to the influence these schools have in passing their values on to students.

In reflecting on the Carnegie Conversation on Catholic Education held at Palo Alto California in fall of 2007, the phenomenon of interest lacking investigation is the culture of the organization itself, which in this case is the Catholic school. Culture must be understood as an active, living phenomenon through which people create and recreate the worlds in which they live. Values, beliefs, norms and behaviors are intertwined to represent organizational culture.

> *In this context the Catholic school possesses a special character and nature which no longer posits it as just an educational organization, but as an apostolate of the Church with its own unique knowledge base.*

Culture is the glue that keeps an organization together; it is the way things are done. Culture articulates ritual, beliefs and values through social relations, customs, curriculum, objects and stories. Thus organizational culture is observable. To paraphrase the *New York Times* editorial the culture of the Catholic school lends itself by its symbols, history, rituals and moral codes to religious formation. Consequently, the Catholic school then is the custodian of a preset of mores combining religious and academic cultures. Conclusively, the Catholic school constructs a particular mission based on values, beliefs, norms and behaviors, and by its very nature it encapsulates organizational boundaries of identity and intentionality. These boundaries, complemented by parents, faculty, students and parish, construct a purposeful faith community of learners.

In this context, the Catholic school possesses a special character and nature which no longer posits it as just an educational organization, but as an apostolate of the Church with its own unique knowledge base. Such an organization requires a hermeneutical application viewed through the lenses of various academic disciplines, such as anthropology, theology, history and pedagogy to allow for social legitimacy. Only then can theories and codified norms lead to rigorous research and standards for best practice. If the philosophical tenets of hermeneutics are not applied in the discernment of the Catholic school as an educational institution, the process suffers from the lack of an epistemological frame. Such conduct relies on isomorphism as a research tool, ignoring contextualization in comparing the Catholic school to the American public school and more recently the charter school.

Moreover, from its beginning the Catholic Church has had as one of its primary instruments of evangelization Catholic schools run by learned women and men: it is a tradition that we as school leaders can lean on. The charisms of the Benedictines, Ursulines, Christian Brothers, Salesians, Jesuits and other religious congregations are regarded even by those outside of our Catholic community as sources of wisdom. Learned women and men in monasteries and universities all lend themselves to a scholastic tradition in the Catholic school. Catholic educators are buttresses with this knowledge as they approach learning and instructional improvements, cognitive development, assessment and testing, evaluation, supervision, observation, and alignment of curriculum to federal, state and local requirements without compromising scholastic leadership. For this reason, Catholic schools with Catholic education is a field of study.

Gerald Cattaro, Ed.D., is Chair of the Division of Educational Leadership, Administration, and Policy and Executive Director of the Center for Catholic School Leadership at Fordham University.

The wrong ruling on vouchers. (2002, June 28). *The New York Times*, p. A26.

A Reflection by Tom Doyle

The presentation by Dan Lapsley, "On the Emergent Field of Catholic Education," poses an intriguing issue: "We know what good education looks like—but what constitutes good Catholic education? What does 'Catholic,' used as an adjective, add to what we know about good education more generally?" The path that he pursues in addressing this question is to pose a second question: "How is child development nurtured in a climate of faith?" This is surely a central question in thinking about the essential nature of "Catholic" education, perhaps the central question, but another question does occur: "What in the Catholic intellectual tradition serves as a ground for a good Catholic education?"

Several thoughts come to mind, but one, in particular, might be instructive: Objective truth exists and whatever its source is to be valued. The implications for the school and classroom are significant. For instance, in the spirit of ecumenism Catholic schools will respect and value other faith traditions in teaching and in practice. Religion classes, while ensuring that all students are competently grounded in Catholic teaching, may incorporate appropriately the insights of other traditions. Similarly, for a Catholic school with a student body that is predominantly Baptist, while Eucharist will remain the central expression of worship, the vivid and energetic prayer tradition of the Baptist experience will be invited into the life of the school. Such respect would be in accord with Saint Augustine, who in *On Christian Doctrine* notes: "but by the command of God...some truths in regard even to the worship of the One God are found among [the Egyptians]" (Bk II, para. 60).

In a non-religious instance the often-cited tension, even antagonism, between science and religion can be a troubling issue for teachers in their planning of curriculum. In a local culture that is persuaded to Scriptural literalism, the inclusion of the study of biological evolution can be a source of consternation or conflict among families and students. Some will argue that even if true, evolution should not be taught because it leads to a weakening of moral thinking. In a Catholic school evolution will be taught, scientifically, not polemically, as will the "big bang theory," while bioethical issues will be discussed thoughtfully with full presentation of the scientific facts and reasoning informed by the moral thought of the Church. In accepting new ideas as objectively true, Catholic tradition, though cautious with good reason about accepting new ideas as true, rethinks its own traditions of truth in the light of stronger evidence.

The principle may be relevant only in particular circumstances, but for those situations it can be a powerful witness to a community about the long-standing wisdom of the Church in thinking about human knowledge, its reach and its limits. Though not as pervasive in its application as the principle that Lapsley suggests in his question, the conviction about objective truth, countercultural in this day of the post-modern, is essential to notions of community and common good that are at the heart of Catholic thought.

Tom Doyle, Ph.D., is the Academic Director of the M.Ed. Program in the Alliance for Catholic Education at the University of Notre Dame.

A Reflection by James Heft, S.M.

In thinking about education as a field, it is important to understand more clearly the meaning of field. Fields of research are interdisciplinary. They are not housed in separate departments, or even in distinct colleges or schools of education. This goal recognizes implicitly the need for research that is different from that which most schools of education and universities currently conduct. Why this shift from departments and schools doing research to creating a field of Catholic education?

A number of answers might be given in response to the question. It might well be the case that too many schools of education at both secular and Catholic universities are not making the difference that needs to be made. It may also be that much of the research that is done currently in schools of education has little relevance beyond those schools and is often based mainly on narrow questions of practice. Other critics of schools of education point out that most education majors, though of course there are exceptions, have low SAT scores when compared to their peers majoring in other subjects, especially those in the sciences. Finally, some critics feel that schools of education at Catholic universities are oriented primarily to the public school systems in which most of their graduates will teach, and for which there is considerably more government-funded research. There is some truth to all of these criticisms. Moreover, it is simply a fact that most schools of education are underfunded and, on the graduate level, often overwhelmed by the number of students who want graduate degrees, not primarily for the intellectual development they might undergo, but rather to increase their pay and rank in the public school system.

Another troubling aspect of this entire conversation is that nearly 90% of Catholic children are not in Catholic schools.

Part of the problem reaches well beyond the schools of education. Given all the options that now face talented students, few receive support from our wider culture in choosing a career in teaching, especially at the primary and secondary school level. Good teachers are neither sufficiently recognized nor rewarded for the critically important roles that they play in preparing the next generation for life and work. But schools of education have another challenge, one that comes not from the wider culture so much as from within the academy itself. It is a pervasive snobbery that infects the academy; I am referring to the unfortunate tendency most faculty have of looking down upon areas of teaching and research that emphasize practice. For example, in my own field, if I may call it that, pastoral theology is often thought to demand less intellectual ability than the other sub-specialties like systematic theology, historical theology, or biblical exegesis. Personally, I think pastoral theology is the most intellectually demanding of all the sub-specialties for the simple reason that it requires not only an overall grasp of all the other sub-specialties, but also the ability to understand the people with whom one speaks, and the culture in which they live. Pastoral theology demands that a person be able to communicate well, all the while offering both catechesis and critical theological reflection. Unfortunately, the academy has been too long dominated by scientific modes of reasoning, and insufficiently appreciative of the importance of practical reasoning—that is, the type of reasoning that bridges theory and practice and deepens their critical interaction. That those in the academy who view academic rigor in this way would look down upon disciplines that bridge theory and practice should not surprise anyone.

How to finance Catholic schools remains a huge problem. John E. Coons, Professor Emeritus of the Berkeley School of Law, and long time advocate of school vouchers, presented a stirring paper at the Carnegie conference. Coons made a number of claims. First, if we make vouchers a Catholic schools' issue, it is bound to fail. Second, vouchers will benefit both public and private school systems. Third, it is crucial to remember that the primary educators of children are the parents, and that they should have a choice, not determined by the state, as to how to educate their children. Philanthropists have stepped up to fund the new models of schools mentioned above—funding that currently amounts to over $80 million. If Coons is right, and I believe he is, then efforts to win vouchers, if they are to be successful, must be bipartisan; they must be supported by leaders in both the public and private sectors. We are obviously a long distance away from that vision of the common good. But it is precisely the argument that Catholics should be making—that is, an argument for the common good, not just the good of Catholic schools. Such a carefully coordinated effort is greatly hampered by the incapacity of existing politically motivated institutions to read where most Catholic actually are—in the political middle.

Another troubling aspect of this entire conversation is that nearly 90% of Catholic children are not in Catholic schools. It should be obvious that Catholic educators should renew and deepen their commitment to Catholic schools as the most effective means of evangelization. But what can be done to improve the religious education of the 90% of Catholic students who are not in Catholic schools? Current forms of parish-based religious education programs have produced only mixed results. Are there ways in which Catholic schools might be able to reach out to the vast majority of Catholic students who are not in them? Are there ways to prepare college graduates so that they can be competent and effective teachers of these students? I do not have the answer to this problem, but I do know that when we beat the drum for Catholic schools, as I have been doing for nearly 40 years, I remain painfully aware of the many Catholic children who for a variety of reasons, often financial, are not able to attend those schools.

One final observation: Many years ago, Fr. Andrew Greeley remarked that if we want our Catholic primary and secondary schools to thrive, we need to do what Catholic universities have done—empower lay boards of trustees with genuine fiduciary authority to take on the responsibility for their well-being. At least in the near future, parish priests will be more and more involved in extensive pastoral ministry, increasingly required to look after not just one but two or even three parishes. The rapid growth of lay ecclesial ministries has been a welcome development. Why should there not be the same growth in the number of lay persons who take responsibility for the schools in which their children are educated? Surely, there are issues of canon law, church polity, and lay trusteeism, to refer back to a crisis in the early 19th century in Philadelphia. But new times require new structures. What is most important is that the best institutional vehicles for the communication of the faith be established and maintained, and whatever alteration in existing laws and policies are needed, let them be made!

What is most important is that the best institutional vehicles for the communication of the faith be established and maintained.

Fr. James Heft, S.M., Ph.D., is the University Professor of Faith and Culture and Chancellor at the University of Dayton. He currently serves as founding director of the Institute for Advanced Catholic Studies at the University of Southern California. He is a priest of the Society of Mary.

A Reflection by Martin Scanlan

The Moral Compass for Catholic Education

Schools are striving to better serve students across multiple dimensions of diversity in our increasingly pluralistic society. In this context, the Carnegie Conversation on Catholic Education served as a seminal gathering to consider future directions for Catholic schools. In the past five decades, Catholic schools in the United States have weathered tremendous changes in student enrollment. As Fr. Joseph O'Keefe aptly stated in his remarks at the Carnegie Conversation, increasingly for these schools "the goal is not so much to provide an education for Catholic children, but to provide a Catholic education for anyone." Yet, many Catholic schools in both urban and rural settings struggle to respond to this call to provide a Catholic education for anyone.

As I reflect upon the power of the Carnegie Conversation, I believe the core tasks for the field of Catholic education are to explore, articulate, and develop the characteristics that make Catholic schools distinctive educational communities for students. Certainly an essential component that distinguishes Catholic schools is their religious character, including rich sacramental experiences and service learning opportunities. Historically, academic excellence and strong communities of learners have also been hallmarks of Catholic elementary and secondary schools. However, at this historical juncture, another distinctive quality of Catholic education is emerging as vitally important: Catholic social teaching.

Catholic schools throughout the United States that are enacting Catholic social teaching serve as bellwethers.

Catholic social teaching makes Catholic schools distinctive learning environments for educating students who reflect the rich diversity of the human family. Catholic social teaching directs these schools to create teaching and learning communities that affirm the human dignity of all, promote the common good, and demonstrate a preferential option for the marginalized. To the degree that these values infuse their policies and practices, Catholic schools are unique teaching and learning communities, different from schools in other sectors, both private and public. A recent publication from the Congregation for Catholic Education (2007) puts this eloquently:

> The [Catholic] school is called to be a living witness of the love of God among us. It can, moreover, become a means through which it is possible to discern, in the light of the Gospel, what is positive in the world, what needs to be transformed and what injustices must be overcome. (para. 46)

Catholic social teaching provides the moral compass for Catholic schools to rejuvenate themselves in this new millennium. The most vibrant Catholic schools are enacting these teachings. For instance, in some schools, boards are creating new funding models so that they can demonstrate a preferential option for the poor in their recruitment and retention of students. In other schools, teachers are becoming trained in antiracism so that they can critique and ameliorate structures that discriminate and assault human dignity. Elsewhere principals are hiring learning consultants and partnering with community organizations so their schools have the capacity to create effective modes of instruction for students with special needs, affirming the goodness of all members of their community. In short, Catholic schools throughout the United States that are enacting Catholic social teaching serve as bellwethers.

As innovative schools continue to welcome students from all sectors of the human family, the field of Catholic education needs to more substantively support these efforts by cogently articulating the praxis of Catholic social teachings.

The praxis of Catholic social teachings joins theory with practice, exploring essential questions: How can we more effectively affirm human dignity in our governance? How can we more clearly demonstrate a commitment to the common good in practices of recruitment and retention? In what ways do we express a preferential option for the marginalized in our mission statements? While leaders within Catholic schools wrestle with the immediate challenges, educators in the broader field are compelled to provide substantive scholarship to help these leaders answer such questions. The Carnegie Conversation on Catholic Education provided an important meeting point on this journey, and Catholic social teachings can serve as a valuable compass on the path ahead.

Martin Scanlan, Ph.D., is a member of the faculty in Educational Policy and Leadership at Marquette University.

Congregation for Catholic Education. (2007). *Educating together in Catholic schools: A shared mission between consecrated persons and the lay faithful*. Rome: Author.

A Reflection by Mary Walsh and Jillian DePaul

At the recent Carnegie Conversation on Catholic Education, some of the core educational areas proposed for the field of Catholic education included curriculum/instruction, educational leadership, faith development and moral formation. This reflection paper proposes another core educational area: support for the learning and healthy development of students. This domain of schooling, often called "student support," is intended to focus on the needs of the whole child by addressing non-academic barriers to learning, such as mental health issues, inadequate health care, family and community violence, and promoting student strengths.

Historically, Catholic schools have understood their mission to serve the "whole child" as including not only the spiritual and moral dimensions, but also the physical, psychological and social well-being of the child. In past decades, parish schools directly engaged this domain by ensuring that students and their families had access to necessary health, social and psychological supports, primarily through their networks in the parish as well as the larger Catholic health and social service communities. Catholic educators understood that human wholeness was inextricably linked to students' development as learners, as members of the faith community and as future citizens. They saw beyond the content of an intellectual education to the valuable but often murkier process of promoting moral character, spiritual formation and healthy development.

Findings from recent research comparing public and Catholic school teachers' perceptions of and responsiveness to students' support needs demonstrate that a commitment to the whole child is still a strength of Catholic schools (Walsh & Goldschmidt, 2005). However, schools' capacity to actualize this commitment is substantially limited by dwindling resources in both schools and local churches as well as by the uncoupling of schools and parishes through mergers and regionalization.

By tapping the rich supports and services available in the community, Catholic schools can form deep and effective partnerships within the community to assist children and families and thereby promote the common good.

In the public education sector, educational leaders are increasingly recognizing the impact of non-academic barriers to learning on efforts to close the achievement gap. Policy makers have begun to advocate for development of approaches that educate the whole child (Azzam, 2007). School leaders are aware that schools cannot address the non-academic needs of students single-handedly, and thus are seeking ways to build partnerships with local community agencies in order to build a web of services that can support children and families. In scattered efforts throughout the country, single schools are experimenting with models of schooling that meet some of the non-academic needs of students (e.g., full-service schools, extended service approaches including after school models, community schools). Systemic multi-school models for the school-based provision of student support are beginning to emerge, most notably in Boston where a partnership among Boston Public Schools, Boston College, and community agencies provides an evidence-based model of student support for approximately 4,000 students (Walsh & Murphy, 2003).

With their historical and explicit mission to serve the whole child, their deep understanding of community, and their freedom from the negative aspects of standardized testing, Catholic schools are well-positioned to serve as leaders in developing innovative models for addressing barriers to learning, modeling the process of integrating student support into the central mission of education, and articulating best practices for promoting the healthy development of all students. By tapping the rich supports and services available in the community, Catholic schools can form deep and effective partnerships within the community to assist children and families and thereby promote the common good.

Much of the philosophy and practice of Catholic schools is unique, including their explicit commitment to serving the whole child—mind, body and spirit. Nonetheless, emerging trends in the education reform agenda have led to a wide recognition that supporting students in a way that reduces non-academic barriers to learning and promotes positive development is critical to improving academic and social outcomes for all students. By developing, implementing, and sharing innovative and effective approaches to serving the whole child, Catholic educators are in a position to effect change on a large scale across public and private sectors.

Mary Walsh, Ph.D., is the Kearns Professor of Urban Education and Innovative Leadership at the Lynch School of Education at Boston College.

Jillian DePaul is a Ph.D. candidate in Counseling Psychology at Boston College.

Azzam, A. M. (2007). Two takes on whole. *Educational Leadership Online*, 64.
Walsh, M. E., & Goldschmidt, E. P. (2004). Meeting the learning support needs of students. In *Catholic schools for children and youth in poverty: Conversations in excellence* (pp. 43-100). Washington, DC: National Catholic Educational Association.
Walsh, M. E., & Murphy, J. A. (2003). *Children, health and learning: A guide to the issues*. Westport, CT: Praeger.

The Role of the
Philanthropic Community

in Strengthening and
Sustaining Faith-Based
Schools and
Developing a
Robust Field of Study

Presentation I: Francis Butler

It is a pleasure to be with you for this discussion on Catholic schools, a focal point of the greatest interest to many of today's private Catholic oriented foundations.

The planners of today's conference asked me to bring a brief thought piece on the role of the philanthropic community in strengthening Catholic education and what resources are needed to make Catholic schools sustainable and accessible. I will, of course, draw upon my experience with the members of Foundations and Donors Interested in Catholic Activities (FADICA), a consortium of nearly 50 private grant making organizations, but in doing so I am not unmindful of the very strong support and interest of many other foundations and businesses in the United States, in the prospering of Catholic education.

At the outset, I would note that the creative edge of Catholic philanthropy today centers on Catholic education. No topic is more influential in drawing the interest of faith-based donors. FADICA's 30-year history and its frequent conferences on Catholic education are testaments to this. With titles like *Catholic Schools and American Cities, Signs of Hope; How to Save the Catholic Inner City School;* and *Catholic Education: New Pathways and New Possibilities*, our members have spent many days with Catholic education researchers, teachers, administrators, to educate themselves on the major forces at work reshaping Catholic education. Individually, they are involved in the Alliance for Catholic Education, and similar teacher service programs, the emerging network of Cristo Rey, Nativity and San Miguel Schools, urban school scholarship programs, and voucher ventures in major cities of the United States. Not a few are proactive participants with their local Catholic schools, helping them to plan, to merge, to manage themselves better, and to work more collaboratively.

The typical Catholic foundation trustee today would be highly conversant on the changing educational environment. The patterns of declining enrollments, school closings of nearly 500 since 2003, the shortage of teachers, the dramatic acceleration of costs, the increasing tuition paid by parents, the continuing shrinkage in parish and diocesan subsidies, the increase in the number of poor, minorities, and non-Catholics served by our schools, the need for better management, and governance, planning and fundraising, and the growing call for more accountability and third party academic validation, and better school leadership comprise the cases in their grant portfolios at the current time.

Perhaps as never before we have the advantage of active and informed major donors interested and involved in Catholic schools. That is a real plus and a tribute to the history of achievement and the religious and social value that these institutions represent. But this new activism also presents a sea of change for Catholic schools. For institutions unaccustomed to the culture of business, the language of social investing, partnerships, quality management, and impact, it can mean unnavigable waters. Add to that the new realities of and complications of qualifying for public funding through federal and state initiatives, and you can easily appreciate that outside help to these schools is urgently needed.

It is my conviction that millions of dollars in private and public assistance are left on the table each year and millions more are wasted through inefficiencies, poor administration, and leadership in our Catholic schools because church resources are limited, oversight is inadequate, and outside help is lacking.

This is where I believe that philanthropy working in partnership with Catholic higher education could make an important difference. Earlier I referred to the variety of ways in which foundations and donors have been involved in supporting Catholic education and creating school choice across the nation. Much of this help is aimed at scholarship assistance and promoting access to the Catholic schools. Too little of these resources are aimed at assessment and measuring what is actually happening in the classroom, the quality of instruction, how leadership is exercised, how teacher training and recruitment is best done, how curriculum development should be handled, and innovation and other areas essential to instructional quality.

That is where the universities and colleges, especially through their centers for Catholic education could work in partnership with major foundations that are interested not just in the survival of the schools but in their striving for excellence.

Those of you who follow philanthropy will know that today's donor is more results-oriented, looking for well-led institutions that are able to measure and validate their progress. Social investing is a term heard frequently in philanthropic circles. Faith affiliation of institutions alone will no longer suffice with donors. Increasing numbers of them recognize what Catholic schools have been able to achieve in the past, but they consider of greater importance the answer to the question: Are they still able to deliver the same quality education under changing circumstances?

This suggests to me that the universities and colleges could form partnerships with both the schools and the foundations. Higher education has the research methods, the ability to measure and evaluate, the teaching, and training capacity that is often missing in the local Catholic school systems.

Perhaps as never before we have the advantage of active and informed major donors interested and involved in Catholic schools.

Would it be possible for universities and colleges to work together to help Catholic schools do a better job of measuring achievement and overall management, staffing, and development of Catholic schools? It strikes me that this would be a desirable way to promote a better system of accountability and quality assurance necessary to compete in today's educational environment. It would also provide major donors, foundations, and businesses with the objectivity and perspective needed to help evaluate and strengthen Catholic schools.

Secondly, I believe that interested Catholic universities and colleges working in a concerted way could be a valuable resource for foundations and donors to stay abreast of innovation and important trends. For example, it is reported that the Latino student population in the US grew by 4.5 million over the last 14 years, but less than 5,000 of these students enrolled in Catholic schools. Economics alone will not explain it, but collaborative scholarly research could.

Thirdly, a partnership of universities and colleges for Catholic education would also make possible the collaboration with newly formed organizations like the National Leadership Roundtable on Church Management which is working to promote cost saving best management practices. Is it conceivable that Catholic universities with sizable endowments could make their investment expertise available to local Catholic school systems, establishing guidelines for example on asset allocations in a way that could be replicable at the local level? Another illustration of collaboration could come in the form of showing how to reduce operating costs by managing school properties differently; more centralized purchasing and recruiting, serving as charter school operators so that configurations could be devised where religious identity is still maintained; helping experiment with approaches to building up the enrollments of urban Catholic schools as they have successfully done in places like Indianapolis by door-to-door marketing.

To sum up then, foundations and donors are more interested and conversant than ever on the future of the Catholic schools and they are more proactive. They are looking upon their grant making as social investing and they are expecting measurable results and a spirit of innovation and continuing improvement.

This is where the university community can be of particular help and where collaboration with the philanthropic community and those working to promote a culture of management excellence in the church could work together for a better future for Catholic primary and secondary schools in the United States.

Francis Butler, Ph.D., is the President of Foundations and Donors Interested in Catholic Activities, Inc. (FADICA).

Presentation II: B.J. Cassin

My presentation today is primarily based on seven years of working with the Cristo Rey High School and Nativity/Miguel Middle School movement.

As in business, all markets can be reduced to segments. The Catholic education segment we concentrated on was inner-city, low-income students. Our foundation decided that the NativityMiguel and Cristo Rey models best met this need. I will briefly discuss the resources that have helped grow and sustain these two models.

Many of the experiences I will discuss today could be applied to other segments such as tuition-based Catholic schools. My wife and I decided to invest in the NativtyMiguel and Cristo Rey schools because we were concerned that too many low-income minority children were not receiving the education they deserve. Today, there are 64 NativityMiguel middle schools serving 4,400 students and 19 Cristo Rey high schools serving 4,800 students. The NativityMiguel schools are expected to grow to 6,000 students per year in 2012, and the Cristo Rey schools intend to educate 12,000 students by that same year.

We have to remember that Catholic education is a brand to be proud of, and we should continue to shout out its achievements.

We are not focused on "saving" Catholic education. Instead, we think Catholic education is a superior brand and has something to offer the nation as it tries to improve its education system. Many philanthropists, including our foundation, are troubled that 30% of American high school students drop out of school and 3 million American schoolchildren attend schools that have failed to meet minimum state standards for several years. We're worried that U.S. students' scores in mathematics are at the bottom of industrialized nations and nations like China and India produce more college graduates than we do.

Because of the crisis in education, there are many donors who want to invest in unique programs that give kids a chance for a better future. Last year the 64 NativityMiguel schools generated $48 million in donations, and the 12 Cristo Rey schools operating in 2006–07 raised $34 million and generated another $15 million in revenue from the Corporate Work Study Program. The schools are raising these funds because of the work they do—providing education to the poor—and using a model attractive to many philanthropists.

How did these schools achieve growth and sustainability? First, Catholic schools have to be of the highest quality. Many public schools are improving, and while the record on charter schools is mixed, there are many high performing charter schools located in buildings once occupied by Catholic schools. Catholic schools need excellent teachers who can instruct a broader range of learners than they had to teach a generation ago. Our schools need programs to assist children who enter school several years below grade level, modern technology, and faculty professional development programs that help teachers keep up with the latest trends.

This is where the Cristo Rey Network, located in Chicago, and the NativityMiguel Network enter the scene.

Both networks set standards, perform collegial visits to ensure quality, and hold training conferences on:
- Best Practices for Teachers
- Development—How to raise money
- Graduate Support Programs

- Leadership—Presidents/Principals meeting
- Board Leadership

In short, the networks provide the template and support for new schools and the continued training resources to aid the sustainability of existing schools.

Second, we need data to know how we're doing. The Cristo Rey and NativityMiguel Networks have teamed with the Center for the Applied Research in the Apostolate (CARA) based at Georgetown University to analyze our students' test scores, retention and graduate rates, to examine costs, and to evaluate fundraising. We slice the data all sorts of ways to learn as much as we can about our schools, and we publish the data on our websites. The data aren't always pretty, but allow our schools to have discussions about ways they can improve teaching and learning, and provide our benefactors an honest look at our strengths and weaknesses. By the way, the Gates Foundation is measuring the effectiveness of their teacher coaching grant given to the Cristo Rey schools by improvements in retention rates and test scores. There's no way to avoid the need for good data in today's philanthropic climate.

This leads me to our third lesson—the importance of transparency. Donors want to know how their investments are doing. They want to be able to go on a website and get all the information they need in order to understand the progress a school is making. I think many parents want this same level of transparency to evaluate the effectiveness of the schools where they send their children. Charter and public schools do a much better job than Catholic schools in sharing their data with the public. We have to remember that Catholic education is a brand to be proud of, and we should continue to shout out its achievements.

The final lesson we've learned is the importance of partnering with universities and colleges, particularly Catholic colleges.

Boston College has provided our foundation and now the Cristo Rey network with office space, allowing us to put more resources directly into starting schools. Marquette established a scholarship program for graduates of Cristo Rey Jesuit High School of Chicago. Notre Dame has given full scholarships to our graduates and has hosted summer NativityMiguel teacher workshops. Saint Mary's of Winona, Minnesota has a scholarship program for graduates of the Cristo Rey Network schools. Loyola University of Chicago assists each summer with the Cristo Rey schools' annual new teacher training program. DePaul provides assistance to the Cristo Rey Admissions Training each fall. And several Jesuit colleges have or are planning to host the Cristo Rey Network's annual meeting of college counselors

There are many other Catholic colleges helping our schools, and we're grateful for their assistance.

Finally, we have found that the philanthropic community can provide what I call "added" value in addition to their financial grants.

The Bill and Melinda Gates Foundation monitors the progress of the Cristo Rey movement and provides valuable input on handling growth. Their encouragement and grant led to the completion of a Strategic Plan, detailing the activities to scale the model to 36 schools by 2012.

B.J. Cassin is Chairman and President of the Cassin Educational Initiative Foundation.

I would like to believe our own foundation brought business practices that helped the progress of these two networks. An example of this would be the feasibility study for new schools that includes the need, community support, and financial requirements. A completed feasibility study becomes the business plan for the new school.

Finally, there is a lot of good will and passion in the philanthropic community for education. We, who are interested in preserving and growing Catholic education, must focus on and support the fundamentals of delivering quality education.

Presentation III: John Coons
Access to Responsibility

This panel was to consider the means best-suited "to make faith-based schools sustainable and accessible." Today, where these schools are in fact sustained, it is by money; nor is there any immediate prospect that the vow of poverty will regain popularity sufficient to alter this. And if money is a necessary condition of a school's sustainability, the same holds true for its accessibility to any particular family. Access entails that additional question: for whom? That issue will be my focus.

Faith-based schools are presently accessible to half of America's parents—those who can afford a tuition that covers operating and capital costs. Where there is more than trivial demand, these better-off families are generally served. Our challenge is to extend choice to parents of the other 30 million children, an outcome that will entail political organization, time, and—as ever—money.

The hope for universal choice is not unrealistic. No legal or economic barrier keeps society from empowering parents with scholarships equivalent to the cost of government schools. In a well-ordered system that respects the integrity of private and religious providers, all schools—including those of government—would become accessible by way of parental choice. There is no want of money; the state simply delivers it into the wrong hands.

Whose hands would be right? The answer might turn upon some abiding consensus among Americans about the ideal education; but nothing of the sort exists. Instead, beyond a minimum of skills and respect for the law, Americans hold strongly conflicting ideas about the form and content of good schooling and, indeed, the good life. Thus, reformers who would encourage private decision need not identify and guarantee some ideal paideia and method. All they need is the confidence to preach the one first principle: the choice of a school is better made by ordinary parents with diverse ideas than by government strangers who lack knowledge and affection for the child and accountability for the bad outcomes. One need not demonstrate that parents are good deciders, but only that they are the best. This is not so hard. In fact it seems the settled conviction of all parents who are well-to-do, and they act on it. Their consistent behavior is convincing; at the very least it imposes upon policy makers the rebuttable presumption that choice by all sane and non-criminal parents would be as close as this society could get to both the welfare of the child and the common good. Shortly, I will claim empirical support for this working principle.

We must probe the question: What happens to the bond between child and parent when choice is present, as opposed to when it is absent?

Unless some other premise justifies disenfranchising the poor, our task, then, is to find and deploy those instruments of law, policy and politics that will make universal parental choice an American reality. By the way, parental sovereignty is a principle that, in orthodox Catholic thought, trumps even the correctness of the particular parental belief. Pluralism is not to be understood as a problem but as a fact of life. The Catholic school is prepared to empower parents of every persuasion or belief that does not constitute a clear and present danger to civil order.

The contemporary cast of the public mind is not unfavorable to empowerment of all families. It is merely grossly misinformed by spokesmen for conscriptive state education whose cause has unwittingly been assisted for 40 years by the rhetoric of the classical economist. For four decades the public has been encouraged to understand school choice almost exclusively as part of the dogmatics of market ideology; choice, goes the mantra, will make education efficient and raise test scores. The unwashed middle of America has found this message credible but both incomplete and abstract. Quite properly they love the market, but they see what Milton Friedman could not: that education is different from airlines and banks. Of course, these same parents, when they can pay, use the market to move their own child to an exclusive suburban school quaintly mislabeled "public"; this civic sounding label has for long distracted the middle-

class conscience from the onus of participation in what is a crude injustice. But some at last have begun to worry about the social consequences of this mechanism that so effectively divides us by class and race while flaunting its democratic halo.

Any practical campaign to engage the mind of the American center must begin by limiting free market arguments to their proper instrumental role. The market cannot be mistaken for the good in itself which is centered in the family and more specifically in the relationship of the child to the parent. The dominant problem in our conversation is not the unsustainability of a school; it is the unsustainability of the family where school has forcibly taken the parent's place. Catholic leaders must begin to see and say this. We must probe the question: What happens to the bond between child and parent when choice is present, as opposed to when it is absent? There is no professional research on this issue. Perhaps this should not surprise. One distinguished school sociologist writes me privately that it would be too hot an issue for the academy.

From personal experience, and projecting from analogous findings of Coleman, Bryk and others, I suspect that the deepest effects wrought by schooling are visited upon the family itself and are a strongly a function of the parental capacity—or incapacity—to choose the provider. Perceived respectively as fate or as volition, the connection to the particular school looms large in the mind and spirit of both child and parent; the experience dominates the child's consciousness five days a week for 13 years. Where his or her school has been chosen by the parent, the benign effect is plainly symbiotic: the parent experiences responsibility and control; the child experiences and interprets the parent as authority, friend, advocate and—if necessary—rescuer from the school, which is merely the parents' dispensable agent. In the process the reality of family is authenticated.

Where, instead, the child is conscripted for assignment to P. S. 202, he or she gradually comes to grasp that parents are in fact unimportant; family and parenthood are neither empowering nor necessary. Marriage is not a commitment that the maturing child will regard as a civic vocation to be accepted as an adult. The parent, meanwhile, recognizing her own futility, accepts the transfer of her responsibility to strangers and her own role as passive spectator. If this hypothesis about the contrary effects of choice and fate is plausible, every citizen needs to worry that the conscriptive form of school assignment corrupts the integrity of the family itself. The reformer will focus as intensely upon sustaining the family as upon saving the school which he should value as the instrument available to the discretion of the parent. I think middle-class Americans, and especially the Catholics among them, are ready to confront these ideas and give them political opportunity.

Nor is this poisoning of parental responsibility the only empirical question neglected by academia, foundations, churches and politicians. In good faith many of them continue to defend their conscription of children of ordinary families as the necessary introduction of the young citizen to a curriculum of common values. My own research suggests that if any such curriculum ever existed it does so no longer; nor could it in so pluralistic a society. The reality is contrary; children are delivered by the state to an intellectual lottery of conflicting ideas (or silence) about environment, chastity, war, guns, economy, gay marriage, animal rights, gender roles—add your own hot button issue. And, as for the fundamental

> *I think middle-class Americans, and especially the Catholics among them, are ready to confront these ideas and give them political opportunity.*

source of the duty—if any—of the citizen-child even to worry about such issues, the school is silent and is required to remain so. What is truly remarkable is that, among the thousand works on curriculum, no commentator has even hypothesized that the ideological curriculum of the state system is chaos, much less done the research to test the reality. The existence of a common value curriculum is simply assumed in order to justify herding the poor. Academics shun the question for the further reason of self-preservation.

My prediction is that the United States Supreme Court will be greatly interested in the empirics of the fabulous "civics curriculum" as well as the corrupting effect of conscription upon the family. The time will come when the drafting of the poor for government schools is once again legally challenged, roughly in 2025. Only if the necessary legal and intellectual groundwork has been laid in our own time by strategic deployment of private and foundation resources, will both law and public opinion begin to grasp that the institution of school choice is an imperative of rationality, social justice and the survival of the family among the working class and the poor.

These ideas—all centered in parents' authority—were not the natural language of those reform organizations that were created in the 1980s to be apostles of free-market economics and the libertarian ideal for the world of schooling. Their message spoke to 30% of the public and will continue properly to do so. But the engagement of the center of American society must and will be undertaken by new voices that speak a new language. Parental sovereignty is a motif congenial to middle-of-the-road Democrats and Republicans, and to churches that serve them and the poor. Happily, there is more than a critical mass of moderate politicians, churchmen and intellectuals prepared to take the stand. The creation of a connecting institutional voice for these centrist minds will be critical to focusing what is, so far, an untapped reserve of moral, political and intellectual energy. Such a voice—persistent, funded and properly managed—could be the catalyst of an effective school choice consensus lead by state and local politicians, clergy, open-minded media, maverick teachers and parents.

John Coons, J.D., is the Robert L. Bridges Professor of Law, Emeritus, at the University of California at Berkeley.

In closing, I turn briefly to the issue of the sustainability of the schools themselves. It must become the primary hope for existing private and religious schools that their service to ordinary and poor families can once again be realized—and now in a more comprehensive way. It may well be that cause and effect here will run both ways. The rescue of our saving remnant of Catholic schools may prove a necessary condition of the secular politics of universal access. The general may depend upon the survival of the particular and vice-versa.

I conclude with one word of warning. In our enthusiasm for universal access, let us never yield to the corrupting notion that the specific promise of Catholic schools lies in their capacity to produce brainpower. As Catholics, we are not intellectual Gnostics and do not worship IQ. If they remain truly Catholic, many, perhaps most, of our schools—as some still do—will seek to serve children who are limited, disabled and dysfunctional. True to itself, the Church will be the instrument of a human perfection that is radically higher than mere genius. If genius proves a by-product, so much the better.

A Reflection by Maureen Hackett

As Francis Butler so clearly postulated in his presentation on the role of the philanthropic community, it would be nearly impossible to find a foundation steward unaware of the vast array of problems facing today's Catholic schools. From declining enrollments and school closings, to the dramatic acceleration of costs and an equally dramatic shortage of teachers, to the need for better management and strategic planning, today's philanthropists face a true dilemma: How exactly might their contributions of time and money best serve Catholic education?

No amount of thought or prayer could provide me with any ready-made solutions to the challenges stated above, but philanthropy is an answer to our Catholic duty and the welfare of our Catholic schools. I would like to suggest one way in which we might begin to plan a healthier future for our Catholic schools.

Every school needs an endowment—a successful, nourishing, life-giving financial base—and not some schools, all schools. If a school does not have an endowment, its leadership needs to create one. If an endowment exists, it must be improved.

Catholic schools need financial endowments in order to ensure long-term stability and to have the funds necessary to compete in the ever-changing educational market. These endowments allow the transfer of money or property donated to the institution with the specific stipulation that these monies be invested, not spent down. Only the earnings of the investments are used to finance the needs of the institution; the principal must always remain intact. When properly managed by qualified expert managers, the endowment can achieve significant growth and provide the financial sustainability vital to every school.

> *…today's philanthropists face a true dilemma: How exactly might their contributions of time and money best serve Catholic education?*

I believe that creating and nurturing these endowments to a sustainable, critical mass can eventually enable schools to attract the high quality administration and faculty crucial to their success as institutions and, at the same time, offer students affordable tuition rates. In the best instances, endowments can allow for fixed tuition costs in spite of rising educational costs. An endowment fund also demonstrates to the faculty and staff that their work is valued, and it attracts potential donors. When there are demands for capital improvements, a well-run endowment allows for investors to contribute either to the ongoing capital campaigns of Catholic schools, or, for those not interested in brick and mortar, to the endowment fund. A financial endowment is not just a short-term solution for survival, but rather a long-term plan for a financially sound future.

These endowments require the vigilant stewardship of passionate, dedicated individuals, even if it means looking for them outside the community of enrolled families. Future investors in such endowments generally look to the leadership of the endowment fund to assess its viability and potential for success. In many cases, significant investments to the endowment will come from foundations, corporations, and individuals who do not have children currently enrolled in the school. However, it is important that the pastor and principal of the school be closely involved in cultivating and soliciting new investors to the endowment fund. These leaders also share the responsibility of nurturing the relationships with investors. Keeping benefactors abreast of their investment and its impact on the school is important not only in maintaining communication, but also in encouraging additional contributions.

The establishment of an endowment fund requires a number of important steps. First and foremost is the creation of a strategic plan, or for some, an improvement of the current plan. The strategic plan provides a vision for the future of the school; specifically, it is a road map to show how it can successfully meet the ever-changing challenges of Catholic education. This visionary map allows potential investors an opportunity to see just how dramatically their own investment might contribute to a school's success. Finally, a comprehensive strategic plan is necessary to ensure that the school focuses on its mission of a faith-filled academic program that is affordable to all families.

It is from such a strategic plan that the operational plan can be designed—a plan that outlines how the school will continue to deliver quality education and faith-filled programs to students and their families. Most operational plans include the resources necessary to meet the basic financial targets of the institution, such as the annual fund and tuition revenue. In most cases the major gifts needed to sustain the future of our schools are not represented in this basic plan. Major gifts comprise the majority of our endowment funds. We need to emphasize the need for major gifts in our development efforts and offer an opportunity for our donors to invest not just in the day-to-day operations, but also in the future of the institution. A major gift program will ensure the continued growth of the endowment fund.

To that end, a marketing plan is necessary as well. Marketing plans serve to clearly articulate the value of a Catholic education. Whether our donors prefer to name a building, a scholarship fund, or a program, we must be prepared to present the opportunity for personalized investment that meets individual desires. Like any home, we must maintain our foundation.

In closing, I firmly believe the future of Catholic education rests upon each and every school's ability to create and grow sustainable endowments. I also suggest it should be the primary mission of the philanthropic community to develop the strategies needed to make these endowments spring to life, or to substantially grow them where they already exist.

> *Catholic schools need financial endowments in order to ensure long-term stability and to have the funds necessary to compete in the ever-changing educational market.*

A Reflection by Darla Romfo

The animating force behind all of Catholic education is the person of Jesus Christ, and the ultimate goal of every Catholic school should be to give each child who enters its doors the chance to have a personal encounter with Him. Many in the philanthropic world base their support for Catholic education on the fact that Catholic schools provide a superior academic outcome, a safer and more loving environment in which to learn and values-based education. It is true that each of these characteristics should naturally and intentionally occur within an institution where Christ is the cornerstone. But these are not the primary reasons for the existence of Catholic education, and Catholic leaders in their efforts to save Catholic education need to be bold in this regard.

On a tour of American Catholic universities, Archbishop J. Michael Miller—then a Vatican diplomat, now Archbishop of Vancouver, British Columbia—offered these remarks on Catholic education: "As John Paul II wrote in his 1979 Message to the National Catholic Educational Association of the United States 'Catholic education is above all a question of communicating Christ, of helping to form Christ in the lives of others.' ...To be integral or 'whole,' Catholic schooling must be constantly inspired and guided by the Gospel....The Catholic school would betray its purpose if it failed to take as its touchstone the person of Christ and his Gospel: 'It derives all the energy necessary for its education work from Him'" (Miller, 2005).

A Catholic school would betray its purpose if it failed to take as its touchstone the person of Christ and his Gospel.

One of the things that often seems to be lacking or is understated in much of the writing and talking about the future of Catholic education is adequate emphasis and attention to this very central tenet. Catholic education is so much more than a field or a discipline. It is a person—Jesus Christ—the Way, the Truth and the Life who entered history, changing it forever. It requires high standards and daily opportunities for students' relationships with Christ to deepen, such as prayer, reading the Scriptures and other spiritual books, Mass, and Eucharistic adoration. If the culture of a school as a whole is going to reflect Christ as its cornerstone, every individual in the building must be able to have personal encounters with Jesus every day.

Catholic schools, unlike their secular counterparts, have the freedom and the duty to base their teaching on the premise that truth may be discovered in both its natural and supernatural dimensions. Again, the late Pope John Paul II put it so well. "The greatest challenge to Catholic education in the United States today, and the greatest contribution that authentically Catholic education can make to American culture, is to restore to that culture the conviction that human beings can grasp the truth of things, and in grasping that truth can know their duties to God, to themselves and their neighbors....The contemporary world urgently needs the service of educational institutions which uphold and teach that truth is 'that fundamental value without which freedom, justice and human dignity are extinguished'" (as cited in Miller, 2005).

These core convictions must inform everything from the selection of principals and teachers, to the selection of course materials, and so much more.

Darla Romfo serves as President and Chief Operating Officer of the Children's Scholarship Fund.

Miller, M. (2005). *The Holy See's teaching on Catholic schools* [Keynote address]. Retrieved June 11, 2008, from http://publicaffairs.cua.edu/speeches/06Archbishop MillerKeynote.htm#_ftnref28

A Reflection by Joshua Hale

Building a Field of Catholic Education: Incentives, Incentives, Incentives

At the onset of the Carnegie Conversation, the concept of a field of Catholic education seemed abstract. So far from the classrooms and schools that conference participants had left to attend the Institute, certainly far from the 93 schools I work with on a daily basis. It was hard for me to let go of the mission I work for: the many families living in poverty who just want a safe place for their children to study and realize a brighter future. I found myself asking, what could this field possibly have to do with building Catholic education and, for my purposes, serving the poor? Would a field keep Catholic schools open, build enrollment and strengthen academic programs? I struggled with this even as Lee Shulman presented the concept in such a way that made me realize I had just heard my best professor ever, and even when Maureen Hallinan eloquently distinguished this idea of a field from a discipline. Nonetheless, I only became more entrenched in my view: "Why are we talking about fields? Let's just get to work," I thought. "Why so many studies?" I wondered. I was convinced as I sat listening to the presentations, on the plane ride home, and for weeks after the Carnegie Conversation that the concept of field was best left to soccer and football.

The idea of field seemed to gain greater clarity and importance.

Yet as much as I struggled with this concept, as days and weeks passed and I had more time to reflect on it within the context of the organization where I work, the idea of field seemed to gain greater clarity and importance.

Big Shoulders was founded 22 years ago, and for most of that history it operated as a pass-through organization, raising funds and then, for the most part, turning them over to the Archdiocese of Chicago to disseminate. In this endeavor—raising funds—Big Shoulders was very successful, with more than $163 million raised since inception. That said, Big Shoulders watched as schools it supported continued to close year after year. During its 22-year history, more than 80 inner-city schools have been closed.

About five years ago, Big Shoulders realized that to continue to meet the organization's mission—providing access for inner-city children to a safe and effective education in a Catholic school—it had to refocus its efforts to make sure the schools not only stayed open but were functioning well and providing a high-level education. Furthermore, Big Shoulders was aware this would not be accomplished by just raising more funds. It would only happen by getting more involved—inviting individuals and organizations to take a more active role working with local school leadership. While this might sound simple, it was a major strategic shift.

Since that time, the relationships Big Shoulders keeps has mushroomed to include university leadership and experts, Catholic school consultants, corporations, foundations, business executives and more. Indeed, Big Shoulders is no longer a pass-through organization; instead grants are made only after much discussion, analysis, collaboration and consideration. Our relationship with the archdiocese has changed and continues to evolve toward an even stronger partnership. Big Shoulders no longer simply serves as a checkbook.

I contend that a field is building in Chicago. While I would like to think that Big Shoulders played a role in this shift, it is more accurate to state that Big Shoulders responded to, or followed, a shift toward taking a more hands-on approach to our work. Donors wanted greater involvement. Principals were asking for active partnership. Big Shoulders watched and learned from universities, specifically schools of education, as they continued to focus greater amounts of their time and resources outside their walls and into classrooms and principals' offices. Organizations like ACE and LU Choice sent recent graduates into classrooms once deemed undesirable, as foundations offered incentives to work with new partners. We learned a great deal.

Is this a field? For what it's worth, I think so. Perhaps a simplistic view, a pragmatic view, but indeed this field continues to attract new partners and challenges us all to be better. It creates friction and leads to conversation, even innovation. There is much work to do, but the foundation is strong.

The result has been quite positive for the inner-city schools here in Chicago. For the second year in a row and only the second year in more than 20 years, all of the inner-city Catholic schools remained open. During the most recent school year, enrollment showed signs of stabilizing. Our Cardinal, who has always been incredibly supportive of the schools, seems more bullish on Catholic education than ever.

I start where I finish, with more questions. I am confident though that, not surprisingly, Lee Shulman and Maureen Hallinan are onto something. I should have known! Admittedly, I have much to learn, but of this I am confident: The field is critical and we cannot build it fast enough. We are behind the curve and we need to move fast. Fr. Tim Scully summed it up best: We need to incentivize people. In order for this field of Catholic education to build, and quickly, we need to incentivize behavior toward creating and sustaining a robust field.

Joshua Hale is the Executive Director of the Big Shoulders Fund in Chicago, Illinois.

Innovative
Models for Catholic School Renewal

A Reflection by Mary Diez, William Henk, and Martin Scanlan

It was indeed an honor to participate in the Carnegie Foundation's National Conversation on Catholic Education. The collection of talented and passionate champions of this national treasure tackled the important themes of teacher and leadership formation, enhancing academic quality, and ensuring the sustainability of Catholic schools. The keynote addresses, panel presentations, and subsequent discussions were uniformly rich, and of extraordinary benefit to the three of us, teacher educators from a Catholic university and college in Milwaukee. Beyond contributing our fair share to the dialogue, we engaged in it with a clear purpose in mind: to seek ideas and strategies that would inform, fortify, and enrich our efforts to provide support for the schools of our local archdiocese. We were not disappointed.

The National Conversation confirmed that our efforts over a six-month period prior to the event were right-minded. During that time, Marquette University and Alverno College had been working toward the creation of a new model for impacting our Catholic elementary, middle, and secondary schools. The model that emerged is founded upon a unique partnership of the five Catholic colleges and universities located within the Archdiocese of Milwaukee—including Cardinal Stritch University, Mount Mary College, and Marian College—as well as the Archdiocesan Office for Schools. The partnership grew out of the needs expressed by local Catholic school principals, presidents, teachers, parents, board members, and community supporters. Not surprisingly, the needs mirror closely the themes of the National Conversation. Just as we suspected, the schools of the Archdiocese of Milwaukee encounter essentially the same challenges we heard were confronted by Catholic schools nationwide.

We are extremely optimistic about the influence that our Greater Milwaukee Catholic Education Consortium (GMCEC) will exert, which is why we use it to center our reflection. Our aspirations go beyond the ambitious goal of exerting a transformational impact on Catholic schools in our large, enormously diverse archdiocese. Our additional hope is to become a national model for ways in which Catholic higher education partnerships can support PreK-12 schools through: (1) the professional development of educators, (2) the transmission and modeling of best practices in faith formation, and (3) the improvement of school organizational effectiveness.

More specifically, we envision working closely with our archdiocese's Office for Schools to provide coordinated professional development programming that is responsive to specific needs. Our pool of educational expertise across the five institutions in the consortium is significant, and in the aggregate, our faculties can provide in-depth training around pedagogical practices that span a wide range of topics. Since preparing education professionals is our core business, we expect to be exceptionally successful, providing the archdiocese with an unparalleled range and caliber of service.

The GMCEC also enjoys particular strength in the domain of Catholic mission, identity, and faith formation. A number of our members have served for several years on an archdiocesan committee that has addressed the ongoing challenges of theological competence and faith formation in Catholic schools. The consortium now provides the natural vehicle to extend the work of the group more in the way of direct implementation.

Our sense is that organizational effectiveness will be the most challenging element to orchestrate. It will require a notable degree of cultural change at the five institutions and depend on the volunteerism of professionals outside of our education units. Our expectation is to garner the support of our five presidents in encouraging the development of a new culture of Catholic faith-based civic engagement. In this new culture, professionals across many areas would offer their services to the archdiocese. A pronounced need exists there for expertise in domains such as marketing, finance, strategic planning, institutional research, fundraising, and information technology—all factors that drive sustainability.

In sum, the GMCEC is an innovative, passionate, and professional response to serious problems in Catholic education in Milwaukee and the nation. What sets it apart is its potential to make a major systemic impact. The distinctive multi-

A pronounced need exists there for expertise in domains such as marketing, finance, strategic planning, institutional research, fundraising, and information technology— all factors that drive sustainability.

institutional nature of the partnership affords an unprecedented level of collective capacity that figures to benefit Catholic schools in newfound ways. Properly resourced, the consortium will change the lives of Catholic school students in the Archdiocese of Milwaukee and beyond. They will experience the academic excellence and faith formation that made our Catholic schools great at the turn of the century, and their parents, parishes, and communities can be assured that their schools will be enduring. We believe that the very future of the Catholic Church depends upon its schools, and we intend to do our best to make them world class institutions.

Sister Mary Diez, Ph.D., is the director of a number of projects at Alverno College related to teacher education. She is a member of the School Sisters of St. Francis, the community of religious women who sponsor Alverno College.

William Henk, Ph.D., serves as Dean of the School of Education and Professor of Literacy at Marquette University.

Martin Scanlan, Ph.D., is a member of the faculty in Educational Policy and Leadership at Marquette University.

A Reflection by John Jordan

NativityMiguel Network of Schools

For a field of Catholic education to be worthwhile, it must provide benefit to practitioners who are educating children in communities and classrooms across the country. The NativityMiguel Network of Schools represents one of the most important and innovative education movements in the country. The Network is comprised of 64 schools, in 27 states, serving over 4,400 students. These 64 schools are entrenched in the mission of Catholic education—serving underserved students in mostly urban areas.

Our students come from the poorest communities in the country. Eighty-nine percent of our students are eligible for free and reduced lunch, 53% are African-American, and 36% are Latino. The NativityMiguel model is working: 90% of our graduates have graduated from high school, compared to the national average of less than 60% for low-income students of color. The majority of these young people reside in single family homes and unsafe environments.

While each of the 64 schools within the NativityMiguel Network of Schools is independent and governed by its own Board of Directors and, therefore, able to respond to the needs of children and families it serves, all of the schools are patterned after the NativityMiguel model which includes the following components:

- Extended school day: Children are in school from at least 8 hours a day to as much as 10 and 12 hours per day, providing a safe learning environment.
- Summer program: Schools offer summer enrichment programs and summer camps.
- A focus on service to an underserved population: 89% of students in NativityMiguel schools qualify for the Federal Free and Reduced cost lunch program, an indication that a family is living at or below the national poverty level.
- Middle school age youth: The vast majority of schools within the NativityMiguel Network of Schools focus on the middle school years, offering classroom instruction as early as fifth grade and continuing that instruction through eighth grade graduation.
- A commitment through high school: One of the most powerful dimensions of the NativityMiguel model is the Graduate Support Program. Through this unique program, NativityMiguel schools help place graduating students in high quality high schools, often helping provide and secure the necessary scholarships and financial aid. Young alumni are mentored through high school, and often counseled on to college acceptance and enrollment.

The strength of the NativityMiguel Network of Schools comes from the strength and uniqueness of its mission, and the willingness of donors to support that mission. Our schools annually raise $52.8 million from foundations, corporations and individual donors. The NativityMiguel Network of Schools has solved the funding problem. This allows our schools to focus on developing an innovative education program that serves our most underserved children.

The NativityMiguel Network of Schools, as innovative practitioners on the cutting edge of Catholic education, will benefit from a strong and vital field of Catholic education. Member schools would benefit in two primary ways: through research and training.

Our model, and others, should be studied in depth in order to give hard scientific support to what we already know anecdotally: This model is working.

The "wisdom of social scientists" will come to bear greatly on our work. Our model, and others, should be studied in depth in order to give hard scientific support to what we already know anecdotally: This model is working. However, we realize that our schools would also benefit greatly from a scientific study of exactly what is working in our classrooms, and why. A researched list of best practices demonstrating what is most efficacious in educating our children will make our schools stronger.

Additionally, our teachers are in dire need of professional development that addresses the specific demands placed upon faculty. Schools struggle to meet the financial needs of keeping their doors open day to day. Substantive and effective professional development feels like a luxury that many of our schools feel they cannot afford. Working in a Catholic school generally, and a NativityMiguel school specifically, is unlike working or teaching anywhere else, and establishing a field of Catholic education would begin to help address this very real need to train teachers to be effective educators and models in the faith.

Further, the NativityMiguel Network of Schools considers it imperative that the field of Catholic education be radically interdepartmental. Financial sustainability will perpetually be a problem facing Catholic schools. By partnering with university business schools, our schools would receive training and consulting services that would help schools strategically consider plans for financial stability and sustainability.

As we consider how best to form a field of Catholic education, we realize that educators, researchers and practitioners must be co-creators. Ultimately our mission is to serve and educate underserved children of our communities. This is a mission that the NativityMiguel Network of schools is ardently striving to fulfill, and one that we will better understand and achieve with the aid of a competent and vital community participating in the field of Catholic education.

Monsignor John Jordan joined the NativityMiguel Network of Schools as Executive Director in October 2004.

www.ingramcontent.com/pod-product-compliance
Lightning Source LLC
Chambersburg PA
CBHW060755090426
42736CB00002B/43